Never give up on your dreams.
The best is yet to come.

Pessef

Losing FAITH

Finding HOPE

By
Jesse A. Cruz

Jesse A. Cruz

http://www.JesseCruzSpeaks.com/

New International Revised Version (NIRV) is the source file for all Bible quotes.

Published by Skinny Brown Dog Media
http://www.skinnybrowndogmedia.com/

Development Editing and Cover Design: Eric G Reid
www.SuccessLifeU.com

Print ISBN: **978-1-7370393-0-3**

If you would like to hire Jesse A. Cruz
as a coach or speaker, please contact him via
http://www.jessecruzspeaks.com

Dedication

To my Lord and Savior, Jesus Christ, the King of Kings. My beautiful Queen Desiré. My two princesses, Haleigh and Mariah, and my forever angel, Faith. Thank you for loving me when I was unable to love myself.

Foreword

In 2019, I was in New York to speak at a child abuse conference. At this point in my speaking career, I was comfortable sharing my story of being kidnapped and raped at twelve years old.

Generally, after I spoke, I would take time to greet those who had been gracious enough to hear my story, then head back to my hotel room to grab a bite to eat. This trip was different as my publisher had arranged for me to do a book signing following my stage time. As I was signing books and thanking guests, Jesse walked up to my table with great enthusiasm. I remember how Jesse introduced himself, and he seemed to have a sense of urgency about telling me something. As I stepped out from behind the table, I was seated at he told me he, too, wanted to share his story with the world. It didn't take long before Jesse started pouring into me his story and his love and passion for God. Jesse's passion and conviction reignited something in me.

In *Losing Faith Finding Hope,* you too will be introduced to Jesse's passion for life and love of God. *Losing Faith and Finding Hope* helps answer one of life's most difficult questions each of us will ask at some point in our lives, "Where is God when the unthinkable happens?" Jesse boldly and authentically shares with us his heart as he struggles to hold onto his faith as his daughter lays dying before his eyes. The courage and love Jesse showed amid uncertainty can help us see the power of resiliency.

After reading *Losing Faith Finding Hope*, I was led to rebuild my relationship with God. Through Jesse's words and witness, I now see God's love and His grace and will be forever changed.

I have gone through personal tragedy and survived, but I never dared to confront the one question that has haunted me. Where was God when I was being raped as a twelve-year-old boy? Thank you, Jesse Cruz, for your honesty and openness, and commitment to telling your story and honor Faith's life in this way. Because of you, I can finally say I am on the road to healing as a man of God. Jesse's story is a testament that God never leaves us, even during the darkest of times. This book will not only change your life it will change the lives of those closest to you.

Kevin McNeil

Author of *The Six Requirements to Be Blessed*

And *Godchild: Why Some Systems Need to be Broken*

CONTENTS

Introduction

Have you ever wanted to break the silence of your anger at God? Witnessing my premature child fight for her life shattered my faith. This book will show you how resilience is possible by turning your pain into purpose. I share my reflections on how I learned how to live again. The grief process does not follow a step-by-step manual to automatic relief; instead, it is a lifelong healing journey. I have spent years reflecting on my experience, and I hope that, this story will give you the courage to begin healing.

This story was initially intended for my daughter Faith and myself. However, as I finished writing this book, I recognized that it could help so many others. If you have experienced loss and desire to take a step forward in your life, allow this book to penetrate your heart and be your guide. Having spent countless hours attending support groups, going through counseling, shedding tears and writing about my experiences, I am confident that *Losing Faith Finding Hope* will do exactly as the title suggests. Despite those moments where you feel like your faith is lost, finding hope is still possible.

FAITH IS BORN

How We Came to Be

I would like to invite you to join me on a journey of healing. To help you understand my story, I will start with how my wife Desiré and I met each other.

I did my best as a single dad to raise my daughter Mariah. I knew I didn't have all the answers for raising a daughter on my own. Although I understood the importance of my role in Mariah's life, I was humble enough to acknowledge I needed help. I believe there are certain things women can do better than men, and one of them is showing little girls how to grow up to become empowered women of faith.

Shortly after I met Desiré, she told me her story and how she and her five-year-old daughter, Haleigh, managed their new reality. Haleigh's biological father, Pete, had been tragically killed before he'd ever had the chance to meet his daughter. The comparison of our circumstances was striking: Desiré had a child who needed a dad, and I had a child who needed a mother. And both our daughters needed a family that understood each other's pain.

Through our unexpected heartbreaks and tragedies, a new family was born. On July 4, 2014, Desiré and I married. On that day we agreed to start a future filled with hope and faith. As we began blending our family, sometimes life flowed smoothly, other times the pill of reality was hard to swallow. The Cruz family learned how to endure challenging seasons that prepared us for seasons of growth and change that we didn't yet realize were ahead of us. Together we persevered through the challenging first years of marriage and began to build a solid foundation for our new family. As we settled into our new normal, Desiré and I often talked about having a baby together.

We hoped that someday we would be blessed with a new baby, but after a couple of years of trying, my faith in that dream started to dwindle. Desiré had been warned that it would be challenging to conceive a child, and she knew she'd beaten the odds when she had Haleigh.

Mariah's faith, on the other hand, seemed to grow stronger despite my fading adult hope. Despite her youth, Mariah has the most mature faith of anyone I know. Every night before bed, she would pray for a baby to be added to our family. Yet as little seven-year-old Mariah began to grab hold of faith, I began to let go of hope.

On August 30, 2016, as she was getting ready for bed, Mariah declared, "A baby will be part of our family soon." She did not say this casually—she stated it with confidence, as a fact, and told me that there was nothing to worry about. I looked her right in the eyes and asked her, "How do you know we're going to have a baby?" She looked back at me with simple clarity and conviction and said, "God already told me."

The News

One beautiful and sunny September day, the Cruz family was changed forever. That afternoon, my girls and I decided to take a bike ride down to the Erie Canal while Desiré went to an appointment. When we reached the park, we took a break to feed the fish. While we were feeding the fish, Desiré called me and politely demanded to know where we were. She told me that she wanted to meet up with us immediately.

After I hung up, two thoughts went through my mind. The first thought was that my wife was checking up on us. The second thought led me to wonder whether I'd done something stupid earlier in the day that I hadn't yet realized- like many men. As I waited for Desiré to arrive, I fully expected her to come to tell me about something foolish I had done. When Desiré arrived, my fears increased: As she walked closer to us, I noticed that she was in tears.

My mind began racing frantically, wondering what I could have done to get her this upset. She walked up to the girls, and then to me. To my surprise, Desiré pulled me in close for a hug and whispered in my ear, "You're going to be a daddy again." Suddenly, I froze like an ice statue, and then melted emotionally. I asked her if she was serious, then quickly realized she would never joke about something we so deeply desired. I wanted to believe she was telling the truth, but I could not envision my prayers coming true in my lack of faith. Without thinking, I said out loud, "But the doctors said you couldn't have another child." In that moment Desiré looked like she wanted to shake me and tell me to stop worrying and start celebrating.

While my weakened faith caused me to doubt her, Desiré decided that hope was a better option.

I still wonder why, when I receive great news, I somehow find a way to doubt. Is it a lack of faith? A loss of hope? Was it because the doctors told us a child was unlikely? I'd begun to believe that the destiny others had spoken over our family would be fulfilled. Once I'd heard someone's opinion about our future, I blindly accepted it as my reality. We had prayed intensely for a child, and now it was finally happening. Yet, even as I was getting everything I'd been praying for, I still found a way to deny it. It was not my belief that had gotten me sidetracked, but my unbelief. To believe the Creator of the universe was taking time to listen to me was unfathomable.

Suddenly, tears filled my eyes with hope—a hope that brought out emotions I had attempted to bury. My head was spinning, and my feelings were rapidly changing. Desiré and I needed to talk more about our miraculous life change, so we loaded up the bikes and headed home. When we got back home, I attempted to process the fantastic news Desiré had just shared with me. I knew our family conversations from this day forward would be different.

I immediately reflected on the conversation I'd had the previous night with my daughter Mariah. She had told me in great faith and with unquestionable confidence that we were going to have a baby. Amazingly, less than twenty-four hours later, her conversation with God became a reality in our family. What we had been praying for over the past two years was finally happening. I thought to myself, "This is truly a miracle." Despite my strong doubts, Mariah's spoken faith and Desiré's news opened the door for me to believe that with God, anything is possible.

Dealing with my stubbornness is a serious challenge for me and can be even more challenging for my wife. It is a blessing that God still loves impatient and stubborn people like me. I foolishly believed that certain prayers were too big for God, but I prayed anyway. I realize now that sometimes I fail to get the results I desire because I lack the faith to think they're within reach and fail to pursue them. Sometimes I can have the greatest faith in the world but lack the action to back it up. Other times I am all action with no faith. With God's power, I can have both.

Full of Faith

Over the next couple of months of Desiré's pregnancy, a vision for our future became etched in our minds. We began discussing names for our miracle child. We started rearranging the house, and our daughters were thrilled with anticipation. Our entire family was full of excitement for the blessing we would be receiving soon. Knowing we would have several months to plan for our new baby gave us a sense of peace. We talked about how this child would change our lives and our family dynamics, and we expressed our fears and hopes.

During an ultrasound, the nurse asked if we wanted to know the sex of the child. With the excitement of kids at Christmas, we said "YES!" As we eagerly awaited the nurse's response, she began to type the answer on the big screen. Before she'd finished typing "It's a GIRL," Desiré and I cried tears of joy. Our dreams were becoming a reality. At the fourth month of the pregnancy, we decided to have a big gender-reveal party with family and friends. As we all celebrated together the news and joy of bringing a baby girl into the world, hope filled our home. Desiré and I enjoyed preparing for our daughter's arrival. Everything was looking great for the Cruz family. Desiré and I had also decided that we would name a baby girl long before we got pregnant. At the time we were unaware of how much our daughter's name would foretell the challenges ahead.

Birth Pains

On a cold January night, my wife informed me she had been feeling deep abdominal pain, which was very concerning, since she was five months pregnant. I thought the pain and discomfort were normal and would pass, but it began to worsen. Over the next two days, Desiré went to the hospital three times. Each time, she was sent home with instructions to "rest and take it easy." I began to feel that something was seriously wrong. After returning home the second time, Desiré became more vocal about the increasing pain and asked to be left alone. I decided to take Haleigh and Mariah over to their grandparents' house for a little while respecting her wishes. Our dog, Bruno, stayed with Desiré, never leaving her side. Clearly, Bruno sensed something was seriously wrong and knew Desiré needed the comfort of his company.

When I returned to check on Desiré, she told me she needed to go back to the hospital. I called Mariah and Haleigh's grandparents to watch the girls a little longer while I took Desiré to the hospital for the third time. After dropping them off, Desiré and I rushed to the emergency room. Desiré was now screaming in pain. The louder she screamed, the more fearful I became. I remember thinking, "I hope she's not going into labor." "Our daughter wasn't due until May."

When Desiré was taken into the room, the doctor confirmed my deepest fear: Desiré was going into premature labor. I dropped my head into my lap. My heart sank like a heavy anchor to the pit of my stomach, and I shed the first of many tears for my daughter that day. The floor became soaked with my sorrow. I knew the chance of my daughter surviving at twenty-three weeks was unlikely, if not impossible. The fear overwhelmed me. Despite my tear-stained face, I tried to stay calm for Desiré. The internal turmoil was slowly crushing me. I believed the worst before my daughter was even born. Instinctively knowing a colossal battle was ahead of us, I immediately reached out to family and friends to pray for our unborn daughter's survival.

The Decision

Four months before her due date, our baby was coming into this world, whether we were prepared or not. When we understood that my wife was in premature labor, we knew we needed to act quickly, so we signed an agreement to be transported to a nearby hospital with a great labor and delivery team. I was certain that if my daughter were born in the ambulance on the way to the hospital, she would have no chance of survival. That forty-five-minute ride to the hospital felt like forty-five years.

Upon arriving at the hospital, I was told that a medicine Desiré could have taken to delay going into labor could no longer be used as she was too far along in her labor. Now we were in a race against the clock. Time appeared to speed up while also going in slow motion.

Have you ever had to make a choice that could result in life or death? This is precisely what we were facing. The doctors asked if we wanted to deliver naturally or by Cesarean section. I asked the doctor what would give us the higher percentage of survival for my wife and our baby. The doctor responded, "If the baby is born naturally, she has a 15 percent survival rate. If the baby is born through a Cesarean section, her survival rate could be as high as 20 percent." These were not the percentages we had planned for. Neither decision give us much hope. We chose Caesarean. That 5 percent difference is where we placed all our hope. As soon as the doctors heard us say C-section, they immediately moved my wife into the emergency surgery room. I was not allowed to follow, and in the rush to try to save our daughter, I did not get to say goodbye to my wife. My emotions went from extreme sorrow to extreme anger.

Praying Against the Odds

Long before Desiré was pregnant, I decided that I would be right next to them when our children come into this world. As it turned out, I could not keep my word in this case. Because of the extreme circumstances, the promise I'd made was broken, and so was I. I felt guilty for not being able to be there for my wife or my daughter. The most difficult thing to do is to let go when you desperately felt like holding on. All alone, I began to wonder how many other situations I would face in the future that would lead me to this crossroad of holding on or having to let go.

My mind began to wander down a negative road. Instead of focusing on the 20 percent chance of life, I focused on the 80 percent chance of death. The internal battle began to breakthrough, and it exploded from my eyes. I did not just cry, I sobbed, and as the tears started to pour down my face, they became my scream for help. I was suffering too much to speak, but my tears did all the talking for me. I did not know human beings could cry this much. After many torturous moments of fear, I began to rage. I thought about destroying the hospital room. I wanted to break everything around me to echo the brokenness inside of me. Instead of what goes up must come down, what is inside must come out.

I decided not to let rage win, but to pray instead. I prayed and I sobbed, and I sobbed, and I prayed. Finally, I picked up the phone and called my mom. As I tried to tell her what was happening, I started crying so hard that I could barely breathe. No matter how hard

I tried to speak, only faint whispers came out. My entire body was shaking. Finally, I uttered, "Will you pray for me?"

Immediately, my mom began to pray for me; as she did, the comforting words from her prayer began to settle me. My sobs and tears no longer flooded me, and I began to breathe again. Panic no longer ruled my body, and peace began to wash over me. My mother's prayer was exactly what I needed. I hung onto every word God spoke through her. As soon as my mom whispered "Amen," I lifted my head, and a nurse entered the room.

We locked eyes. Anxiety was erupting inside of me as I waited to hear what her next words would be. I knew she would share one of two things: my daughter is dead, or she is alive. The pause in the room echoed with a thunderous roar. The nurse finally broke the silence: "She's out; we have her in an incubator." My heart skipped a beat with joy. I was going to meet my daughter. By keeping faith in God and the fantastic doctors, our daughter was alive. On January 6, 2017, our daughter Faith was born.

Loving Through Fear

Getting up from the chair I had melted into, I regained feeling in my body. I wiped away my tears and obediently followed the nurse. I became more impatient with each stride, knowing I was being brought closer to my daughter for the first time. In the distance I saw an incubator holding my precious daughter. As I walked closer, I met the doctor who had been caring for her. Right behind the doctor was my daughter. Finally, I laid eyes on her.

At that moment I felt both joy and numbness. When I saw her tiny body, a sense of awe swept over me. The doctor was talking, trying to inform me of many different details, but I couldn't hear a word he said. My eyes and attention were glued on my daughter. This first meeting was nothing like I had imagined. The doctors and nurses wheeled the incubator into the Neonatal Intensive Care Unit (NICU). It all felt like a dream, but a part of me knew this was really happening. Together, my daughter and I journeyed through a labyrinth of blindingly bright, orange hallways until we finally arrived at what would become Faith's room.

I desperately wanted to pick Faith up. I wanted to hold my baby, hug her, and kiss her, but I could not. There were tubes, wires and monitors coming from all over her body. I knew underneath all the tubes was my beautiful one-pound daughter, Faith. Being her daddy brought warmth to my spirit. I just stared at Faith and thought, *WOW! What a beautiful angel I've been given. My daughter Faith!*

After spending some time with Faith, the nurses told me I should return to the hospital room where my wife was. It was then that I learned she was still unconscious from the anesthesia. As I waited for Desiré to wake up, I couldn't wait to tell her the good news that our daughter was alive. Despite the challenging circumstances, my gratitude for Faith's survival seemed to overpower my fears. When Desiré awoke, she was confused about where she was; but she asked if the baby was okay once she was finally coherent. After I told Desiré that Faith was alive, we embraced each other.

Joyful Grief

After another hour, Desiré was strong enough to get out of bed to make her first walk to visit Faith. As we slowly made our way to the NICU, I felt as if my life had become a dark cave, with only a small candle to light my path. I felt at any moment the guiding flame would flicker out, bringing complete darkness to my life. I had incredible hope, but the unavoidable pain was attempting to drown it out. As we took each step toward our baby, we were unsure if she would still be alive when we got to her.

My tears began flowing with a blend of grief and joy. It seemed crying was becoming a new normal. Despite the assurance from the doctors that Faith was doing alright, I was skeptical. I wasn't sure if the words were true or simply to comfort us. Nevertheless, I decided to choose comfort over truth for that moment.

LIFE IN THE NICU

Wash Your Hands

With all its rules and procedures, the NICU seems to hold most sacred one rule in particular: Wash your hands. As the days passed, every time I stepped up to the large sink to wash my hands, I thought to myself, *I don't want to wash my hands; I want to see my daughter.* This routine, although necessary, was frustrating because it took precious seconds from my time with Faith. This maddening delay also ignited another frustration: Where had these precautions and rules been when my wife had gone to the hospital over and over in unbearable pain?

What if the doctors had listened to her? Would Faith's survival rate be dramatically increased? I thought, *Is my time at this sink supposed to make up for the blood on their hands?* I felt confident that Faith's health would not have been as high risk with the proper precautions. No matter how much I scrubbed my hands, my bitterness could not be washed away.

Every splash hitting the sink was a reminder of the moments I would not get to enjoy with Faith. My handwashing became briefer as time went on, and on days Faith was struggling, soap became optional. I began to envision ripping the sink out from the wall. I didn't need any more water or soap—I only wanted to be cleansed by spending precious moments with Faith.

Helpful Chaos

When we finally made it past the hand-washing station, we were able to turn right and make a mad dash to our daughter. Arriving next to her isolette, my wife laid eyes on Faith for the first time. Faith's beauty was illuminating. Together we cherished our first moments with our baby as mom and dad.

Doctors, nurses, counselors, clergy and volunteers kept coming in and out of Faith's room minute after minute. It all felt like madness to me. I just wanted to spend alone time with Faith, but her needs required a team of people to keep her alive. Our lives were quickly being interwoven with strangers. I wanted to scream for all of them to leave, but silently prayed for them to stay. My anger was becoming unhealthy, and I knew I needed to remain quiet and let silence replace the noise.

As we spent time in the NICU, Desiré and I would talk with the team and answer any questions they had during shift changes or when the doctor would come by. During our brief moments without family and well-wishers, Desiré and I cherished our time alone with Faith. Despite living in the chaos, my wife and I seemed to grow closer. We knew we could not lose hope, even if it felt like Faith was leaving us at times. I would embrace my wife with deep heartwarming hugs while I was too afraid to embrace my baby girl. I learned that any sudden movement would cause Faith pain. I wanted to smother Faith with my love, but the NICU staff told me the best thing I could do was give her space.

Without knowing what to do, I would sit and cry while I prayed. My doubts began to intensify, and the fear of the unknown was starting to take over. Only during times of prayer was I able to feel some level of relief. I needed to know that Faith was going to be okay without knowing if I would be. I was learning that despite how much I demanded, requested and begged for answers from God, he wouldn't necessarily give me clear solutions. It was in the waiting for answers where my faith and hope were being tested.

The Wisdom of "I Don't Know"

Although my experiences are different from most other parents', I believe we can relate to each other no matter what. Why? According to the Centers for Disease Control, 10 percent of children are born prematurely. Statistically, one out of ten parents you know have had a premature baby. I share the statistic not to scare you, but to prepare you.

Since there was only one bed in Desiré's hospital room, I often tried to sleep sitting upright in the chair. I found myself waking up several times in the night with overwhelming discomfort. Wearing the same clothes for two days and not brushing my teeth was not helping my situation. While we stayed at the hospital, we were blessed to have family look after Haleigh and Mariah.

An afternoon came when I finally felt like I could leave Desiré and Faith's side for a couple of hours to go pick up Haleigh and Mariah. Arriving home, I decided it was best for me to be upfront about Faith's premature birth. I looked directly at the girls and said, "Your sister has been born." They didn't believe me. My voice grew deeper as I became more serious and repeated, "Your sister has been born." This time they believed me. Immediately they became filled with excitement. They quickly got ready to go to the hospital to meet their new sister.

During the drive to the hospital, Haleigh and Mariah had so many questions, and I had so few answers. The ride was not our usual car ride, filled with chatting, laughter and music. It was an eerie silence mixed with questions. I'm the type of person that must have an answer to every question. During this drive, I realized that there was no room for pride. I had to answer question after question with "I don't know." I learned that "I don't know" was one of the wisest things I could say at that moment.

By responding to their questions with "I don't know," I authentically acknowledged to my daughters that I don't have all the answers. Knowing what you know and knowing what you don't know is invaluable. Nevertheless, I was frustrated with my ignorance, and that I, too had so many unanswered questions. I wanted to know why Faith was born early, why Faith was fighting for her life, and why this happened to us? But I learned that some questions would not get answered until I've moved on from this world.

The more the girls expected me to know, the deafer I became. I couldn't stomach the thought of them going through the horrific experience of losing a sibling at such a young age. I wanted to protect them and tell them everything would be okay. Yet I knew that wanting things to be okay doesn't simply make them okay. At this moment, things were awful and uncertain, and I just couldn't muster up the courage to tell them this truth. Suddenly Mariah and Haleigh's voices began to fade. Despite not being in the hospital, all I could focus on was the beeping sound from the NICU. I asked myself, *Will Faith be alive when we get there?* I didn't know.

The Uncomfortable Introduction

When we arrived at the hospital, I showed Mariah and Haleigh the process of going into the NICU and the hand-washing requirements. The NICU required that I wear an ID badge. Having to wear that badge in the hospital caused me mixed emotions. I was in deep grief because wearing the badge represented that my child was in grave danger. Everyone knew when they saw my badge that my child might not survive. Yet a part of me wanted to proudly display it to the world, because that badge signified a second chance at life.

Upon entering the NICU, the girls and I made another long walk through the halls. What I saw troubled me: baby after baby fighting to survive another minute. This was one of the saddest experiences of my life. In this NICU hallway, death was normal. I wanted my daughter to be the exception.

I am an affectionate father. Hugs and kisses and cuddles with my daughters are in my nature, but now I wasn't able to do that with Faith. I knew the space she rested in was vital for supporting her healing, yet all I wanted to do was to remove her from her that isolation. I just wanted to hold my daughter the way a dad is supposed to hold his child. Instead of holding her, all I could do was hold back.

More than anything, I wanted to assure Faith everything would be alright, even if deep down I knew it might not. The physical barrier between my daughter Faith and I weakened my ability to form an emotional bond with her. Without being the dad I wanted to be, I was lost on what to do. I was frozen in fear. Faith's failing health was a repeating loop in my mind.

Arriving at Faith's room, I was relieved that her condition was stable, yet saddened that she showed no improvement. The conversations in my head were tortuous. I was unaware I could grieve something I still had. I still had Faith, but her unstable health was frightening me to the core. I couldn't believe she was fighting for her life. Even though she was alive, I felt that at any moment she was going to die.

Nearly overcome with internal turmoil, I finally mustered up the courage to speak to the girls. Haleigh and Mariah had waited silently, taking cues from me on what to do next. As we looked at Faith, I found myself starting to cry and looking at Haleigh and Mariah. With their eyes of hope, I began to make the introduction: "Haleigh and Mariah, this is your sister, Faith."

The Miracle of Faith

With each visit the girls had more questions we could not answer. But all the unanswered questions could not stop Haleigh and Mariah from staring at Faith in amazement and curiosity and sisterly love. Eventually, we all got comfortable being uncomfortable in this new, unfamiliar family space. During all the craziness we tried just to be a family for a few brief moments. As soon as we got comfortable, another nurse, doctor, or respiratory team member would come in and unsettle everything. In the middle of all of this, a researcher asked if we would allow him to use a specific cloth to provide our daughter with some protection and improve her chance of recovering. We thought if this magic cloth could help Faith, we wanted our daughter to have it. That day our time together with Faith felt like a constant exercise routine, with all the moving we had to do to make room for the hospital team. Soon we started to develop a rhythm while being with Faith. Desiré would pump milk to breastfeed Faith, we would play worship songs in the room, Desiré and I would take turns reading to Faith, and then the girls would read to her. For the girls, reading was an opportunity to be a part of Faith's healing, and it was something they were proud to be able to do.

One afternoon, Desiré shared a conversation she'd had with a nurse who told her about Faith's delivery and the doctors' decisions. Desiré was startled to learn that a baby must be at least twenty-three in gestational age at the time of delivery for there to be an expectation of survival. Faith made the cut-off by two days. Even more shocking was our discovery that when Faith was born, she was delivered still inside the amniotic sac. In all her years of delivering babies, the nurse said that she had never seen this before. Indeed, Faith was a miracle! Desiré was encouraged to know our daughter was special and memorable to us and others.

I, like others, have my ideas about how my life will turn out. Regardless of what I believe, faith will influence the trajectory of your life. For those who want faith to happen in a straight line, the more crooked the path seems to become. For a control freak like myself, faith is even a more troubling concept. I believed when my daughter Faith was born, she would be born at nine months, like most babies. I believed she would live a normal life. I learned faith is not like most things, it is uncommon and unique, and faith can be challenging too. Faith does not show us the finish line, but it does provide a clue on how to reach our final destination.

LIFE SUPPORT

Ronald McDonald House

After I'd spent five days sitting all day and trying to sleep at night in a chair in Faith's room, someone from the hospital staff suggested we go to the Ronald McDonald House. At the time I knew nothing about the Ronald McDonald House. What I came to find out was that Ronald McDonald House Charities is a nonprofit organization with a mission to "Create, find and support programs that directly improve the health and well-being of children and their families." Their vision is "A world where all children have access to medical care, and their families are supported and actively involved in their children's care." I connected deeply and immediately with the idea of an organization that focuses on, "Thinking globally, acting locally to provide resources for children and their families."

Walking into the Ronald McDonald House, I was frightened, but I quickly grew comfortable being in such a healing environment. Desiré and I were able to build relationships with other families who were going through similar situations. My family was fractured, and I was determined to heal us and bring us together again. I found strength in witnessing other families learning how to cope and find hope in all the uncertainty. It let me know that I was not alone. I was comforted to know we weren't the only ones walking around with unhealed wounds. During our time at the Ronald McDonald House, I learned that pain is more bearable when surrounded by others who are healing from similar hurts.

While pain isolates, healing leads to community. At the Ronald McDonald House I learned that everyone who is hurting needs a place to connect with others who can provide a healing environment. Overcoming the impossible was God's plan for me, as it is for all of us. Many things are impossible to do by my strength, but with God, the impossible becomes possible.

The Ronald McDonald House became a safe place while we were away from our home. During the days spent living in two worlds, I tried my best to give Haleigh and Mariah as normal a life as possible. During the school week I would drop them off at school, then go to the hospital all day to be with Faith and Desiré. In the afternoon, I would leave the hospital to pick up Mariah and Haleigh from school, go back home, make dinner, help with homework, and tuck the girls into bed. On weekends, we all would live at the Ronald McDonald House and travel back and forth to the hospital to be with Faith.

I began to think about past family trips to McDonald's. Happy Meals were all we focused on while I casually tossed change into the donation bin. I was not wholly aware of everything the Ronald McDonald House did. I knew it was an organization that helped people, but I never imagined our family would become a direct beneficiary of any of those contributions. The Ronald McDonald House is more than a house; it is designed to provide comfort and shelter to families and kids fighting a terminal illness. Since experiencing that comfort, every handful of change has taken on a whole new meaning to me. If you are seeking to be generous and charitable, I strongly recommend giving to the Ronald McDonald House. Giving takes on a whole new meaning when you have benefitted from other people's generosity. As I reflect on tossing pocket change into the bin at McDonald's, I am still amazed. I learned that pocket change has the power to change lives.

Paralyzed by Pain

Every time we returned to the hospital, the hospital staff would update us on Faith's condition. "Doing well" was a standard progress report for the first couple of weeks. After a while, I didn't know if I should trust the "doing well" report anymore, especially after learning that NICU babies show either a significant improvement or a big decline after the two-week mark. Hearing this, I was unsure if I should celebrate or grieve or just hold my breath. Moment by moment and breath by breath, when I sat with Faith listening to her breathe, I couldn't help but think her next breath could be her last. The NICU team told us the journey would be like a roller coaster, with rapid ups and downs, and I just need to buckle up and try to hold on. I was just hoping God would give me an airbag before I self-destructed into despair on this roller coaster.

I know the Bible says we will be tested, yet I struggled with why my daughter had to struggle so much. I thought there must be some better method for testing me.

Pain has a unique way of providing focus. Faith's pain brought me pain, and nothing else mattered. Anything that happened the day before did not exist anymore in my brain. Anything that possibly could occur the next day could not be processed in my need to say present with Faith. I didn't have time to worry about social media, the news, the economy, politics, or anything else.

I finally came to realize that all of my sufferings could either lead me to the unanswerable question of WHY, leaving me in despair, or to the question of HOW—as in, How will I repair and rebuild my faith and my family when this is all over?

Supportive Strangers, Distant Friends

During this hardship, Desiré and I were blessed with overwhelming support from others. We had always made it our mission to serve others and give to others as best as possible. Yet when it came time for others to help us, I struggled to receive it. I didn't know how to still my ego and accept the generosity of others. Nevertheless, I was grateful for all the people who sent cards, money and gifts, prayed for us, cooked us meals, and watched our children.

I found it most disheartening that some of our family and friends grew silent and didn't reach out to us. The people I most expected to step up instead took a step down—and some even took a step out of our lives. Maybe someday I will be able to give grace to the ones who appeared not to care. Perhaps some of them had their pain to deal with and could not help me in mine. Maybe some may have been just too scared to be faced with death and their mortality.

I became grateful for everyone who reached out to us. Some people who were only acquaintances or strangers stepped up and supported our family in unexpected ways. Those acts of generosity changed our family forever.

Learning About Prayer

I welcomed the prayers of others, and I prayed more than ever before. I had to learn how to listen to what God was speaking into my life. When I prayed, I tried to remember prayer is a two-way conversation. I need to not only talk to God, but give him my undivided attention and listen to what he wants to reveal to me. Sometimes his answers do not come as a whisper in my spirit, but from other people or circumstances that move my spirit into action.

In the past my prayers were mainly focused on complaining, trying to bargain with God, or demanding that he do things my way. This is not the way to pray. Because I failed to surrender completely to God, my prayers were not genuine. Prayer only became real when I gave up control and left things in God's hands. When I put my worries into God's hands, I don't need to pick them back up. If I do, then I haven't truly handed them off to God.

Over time I came to the point where I could release my need to control the future, and I was able to communicate with God more clearly. I started to see that prayer needed to be followed with action.

Every ounce of support and encouragement I received was from God working through other people. Through the generosity of others, I was being empowered to experience God's presence. Some people learn life lessons through times of beauty, but it was during times of darkness when I saw his light of love.

The "Weight"ing Room

Each time I walked through the NICU and saw all those babies fighting for their lives, I became sick to my stomach with grief. With each step I took, it was as if my heart was being weighed down with the agony of shattered lives. Instead of a waiting room for healing, the NICU felt like a holding zone for death. I now know why they call it a waiting room, because while I waited, the weight of the unknown ending to this grief was crushing me. Sometimes I've foolishly depended on undependable people. Other times I have depended on myself. If I had fully allowed God to help me carry the weight I was holding on to, this endless waiting room would have been filled with peace instead of fear.

I know we all carry some form of grief with us. If we don't grieve properly, the weight of that grief becomes unmanageable. The added weight of a bad decision is more difficult to carry. But when grief is carried in healing, it creates new strength in our character.

Have you ever been to a gym and used a spotter? A spotter is someone who supports weight while you are attempting to lift it. Any time I try to be strong on my own, I fail miserably. Trusting God gives me the strength to get through any adversity. I finally began to realize that I needed God to be my spotter as I tried to lift this weight of grief from my life.

God, Where Are You?

As I grew closer in my relationship with God, I began to wonder where God had been through all the chaos. I questioned how a loving, powerful and just God could allow my daughter's suffering to happen. I began to wrestle with my concept of God, realizing that God is too big to fit into the box I'd tried to place him in. God is so amazing that no theologian, pastor, or atheist can genuinely define him. God is so beyond our limited understanding—who was I to try to figure him out? It was my doubt of God that drove me to dig deeper into my faith journey. I decided then that if God could be defined completely, then God could not be God. No matter how I feel, I know God is love. Because I cannot fully understand God, nor can I truly grasp how much God loves me.

My awareness of God's presence increased with each walk through the NICU hallway. I began searching for the light only after I'd been in complete darkness in my flawed nature. Grasping for hope while facing my daughter's death every day brought me into full awareness of and dependence on God. Like many people, I typically wait until a crisis has happened to lean on God. Truthfully, if I would depend on God in life's daily routines, all my experiences would be filled with peace and purpose. Although I might never understand why Faith had to suffer as she did, I knew in my heart God is real and God is good, even when life feels awful. I recognized that God not only exists during my brightest moments but is nearby during my darkest pain.

Let Her Breath!

No event in my life, including death, can or will change the existence of God. Yet despite acknowledging this truth, my emotions began to trick me. I became righteously angry at how unfair it was that my innocent daughter had fallen victim to a potentially terminal health condition. As I read John 16:33, "In this world you will have trouble," I thought that if I could be good enough and "Christian" enough and do more good deeds, then somehow, I would be excused from life's challenges. Yet if Jesus himself, who was perfect, was not exempt from pain and suffering, it was foolish to think my family, or I would be spared pain and suffering.

When Faith was 30 days old, her doctors no longer said she was "Doing well." Today's report was that her condition was not improving, and her breathing had started to become shallower. A silent rage of war against God's injustice waged heavily on my mind. I began to cry out to God, "Haven't we been through enough? My child is suffering and can die at any moment. Where are you? Let her breathe!" My fear became paralyzing. I thought God had forgotten about me. Of course, I knew God does answer my prayers, although I may not always like his response. Like any parent, God responds to his children's requests with one of three answers: yes, no, or wait.

If you are hurting, I encourage you to reach out to God; I promise he hears your prayers. God did not forget about you. God is listening, and he still cares. The answer you are seeking can appear in a few days or weeks, but for some of us it can take years, for others, a lifetime. No matter how long it takes, never stop praying, because God never stops listening. When I cried out to God to save my daughter, he did answer my prayer, but not how I expected.

The Power of Proverbs

Although Faith was breathing, every breath was from a machine. I was hoping she would be able to breathe on her own by now. While sitting with Faith, I began to read the book of Proverbs to her. While reading to her, I noticed something remarkable. Her oxygen levels improved as I kept reading. Reading Proverbs to Faith became a part of her treatment plan. I cannot explain it; I just know what I experienced. My goal was for her just to start breathing easier. I think God's intent was for me to participate in helping Faith heal. In my heart I heard God say he wanted me to exhale Scripture into Faith. The book of Proverbs was not only helping my daughter Faith heal, but it was also helping me heal. Whenever anxiety took over in my body, reading God's Word helped me catch my breath. When I read Proverbs, I connect with God and remember the beautiful memories I shared with Faith.

Super Mom

The constant crisis of Faith's health began to wear me down. I recognized that life's challenges expose the foundation on which I stand. Just when I thought I could put my feet on solid ground, another earthquake of despair would shake my world. When that earthquake stopped, I would often step into quicksand. I felt as if I was one breath away from suffocating in misery. Not knowing if Faith's next breath would arrive, or if her heart had the will to keep fighting, left me hanging by a thread.

Each passing day presented a Goliath of adversity I needed to defeat. For me to have great faith, I needed to push past doubt, yet be willing to accept the outcome. As I struggled through unfamiliar situations with unknown outcomes, my faith became stronger. My daughter Faith kept fighting, and I kept fighting alongside her.

God provided the best doctors to take care of my wife and Faith's needs. Desiré showed as much attention to detail in caring for Faith as the nurses did. With the help of the NICU nurses, Desiré learned how every monitor, wire and machine functioned. Armed with that knowledge, she began to understand what all the numbers on the monitors meant and what ranges they needed to be in for Faith. Relentless in her focus on keeping Faith alive, my wife watched the machines closely, and even learned how to adjust every connected piece of equipment on Faith's body. She became so proficient at this task that she could act quickly to make any necessary adjustments to the monitors herself, without any staff in the room. It was humbling to see her dedication to our daughter.

Once when a new nurse came in and was working with Faith, Desiré turned to me and said, "I don't think she knows what she's doing." Often the new nurse was nervous because our daughter was the most premature baby in the entire hospital. This left my wife feeling uncomfortable with Faith's care, so she would often step in to assist. This was just my wife doing what she always does: following her instincts and communicating her expectations. When she was able to point out things the nurses were unaware of, I knew she essentially had become a nurse, without all the textbooks and student loans.

Desiré's high standards can be intimidating to most people—especially to me! During the first few years of our marriage, she held me to a higher standard than anyone ever had. At times I would become upset and defensive. I resented what I believed to be unreasonable expectations she would place on me. I often grew tired from trying to keep up with her high standards. Looking back, I now see that those expectations are what kept our marriage thriving. She challenged me to be a better husband, father and man. Desiré can push people to their potential. Her gift of being a quick learner makes her an even more effective teacher. The same high expectations that used to exhaust me now refresh me.

Witnessing Desiré's high commitment to helping Faith gave me hope because I could see how God had gifted her to care for others. I've often thought that if everyone could be more like my wife, this world would be a much better place. Desiré held every medical professional to an extremely high standard, and she challenged them when necessary. The staff was receptive to her insights and suggestions. The same standards I had once thought suffocated our marriage were now keeping our baby alive.

Despite her vulnerability, Faith reflected her mother's perseverance. All the doctors and nurses commented on Faith's feistiness. When Faith moved, she moved aggressively, clearly telling the doctors when she was uncomfortable. She was a fighter with incredible strength.

Desiré educated me on everything in the room. I remember thinking, *Wow, she's brilliant. Here I am, like a deer in the headlights.* I couldn't even push the privacy curtain forward without struggling. Without Desiré, I don't believe Faith would have been cared for with such attention.

My greatest hero is my wife. I try my best to thank Desiré as much as possible for all she does.

GOD IS WITH HER

Picture the Future

After experiencing another day of struggle, followed by miraculous improvement, Desiré and I decided to take a break. Our emotions were again at the mercy of the roller coaster called the NICU life. We decided to go downstairs and get lunch with empty tear ducts from a storm of feelings we had just released. On the way to the cafeteria, I saw a vast, beautiful photograph. The photograph was a picture of a father holding his newborn infant in his hands. Just when I thought I had no tears left to cry, as I looked at the picture, the tears resurfaced.

I looked at Desiré with mixed feelings of joy for the father and emptiness in my fatherhood journey. I said, "I hope that someday I can hold her." I just wanted to hold Faith the same way the man in the picture held his baby. Yet, it was not an option at that moment. Desiré assured me that someday I would. I became fixated on that photo because it showed not only what my daughter needed but also what I needed.

That image also caused me to realize that I, too, needed a father to hold me safely. Isolation had crept in, and at that moment, I felt like an orphan, hoping for a father to hold me. Even if I had both my parents with me right now, they would only be holding me for a few years. My eternal Father will hold me forever. This thought freed me to stop looking at my daughter as if she was only MY daughter. She was God's daughter too. God's daughter was suffering. I came to think of Faith as OUR daughter, for now God and I were co-dads for Faith. God generously gave the Cruz family three amazing daughters, and that is a reason to celebrate.

Although God never stopped loving me, it sure felt like it. I needed to know I mattered, and that I was not forgotten. I figured Faith was thinking, *My father doesn't love me; he hasn't picked me up or held me.* Nevertheless, during these dark days, God's love became more real than any love I have ever experienced. His presence was not simply a physical one but a spiritual presence that led to a physical experience. There truly is no love like God's love for me.

How could one photo hanging on a cafeteria wall cause such a moment of reflection? The way God works is beyond my understanding. It is impossible to expect our finite minds to have a complete understanding of an infinite being. Situations and people can point us toward God; however, we need to do our best to trust and follow his plan, even when we do not fully understand what it is. As I considered my heavenly Father's love for me, I couldn't help but become overwhelmed with emotion. Just as I longed for the day, I would be able to hold Faith. I sensed God was waiting for the day I would embrace my trust and faith in him.

My hopes and dreams were focused on Faith's healing so that someday I could hold her as the father was doing in that photo. Desiré's hope was also in Faith's healing, but she was equally willing to accept that her healing might only be complete in heaven.

Be A Kid -No Kidding

The Cruz family spent family time differently than most of the world during our days at the hospital. We spent most of the day concerned about Faith's health. The girls and I would go to the hospital and read to Faith. I would find myself snapping photo after photo, not knowing if this was our last picture together as a family with Faith. These were not my idea of family photos, but they were the best I could do. The emotional exhaustion was thick in my spirit. Mariah and Haleigh were young and needed some time away from the hospital to be children. The hospital staff told me about a playroom upstairs that we were welcome to use if we needed a break. Mariah, Haleigh, and I decided we would check it out to have some fun time for a change.

The hospital playroom was bright and airy, with thirty-foot-high ceilings and beautiful stained-glass windows that painted the walls and floor with a rainbow of colors. There was plenty of space to play games and just run around being silly. For the first time in over thirty days, I cracked a smile and laughed. I had forgotten what it felt like to be happy. I did feel some guilt for enjoying myself. Despite the guilt, I had fun. I did not realize how refreshing it was to relive your childhood with your children. We played basketball and other games, enjoying the competition against one another. For the first time since entering adulthood, I felt like a child. My children brought me into their world and brought me up out of my worry.

The playroom became an excellent outlet whenever we needed a break. We became creative and invented our games. Those moments in the playroom and the memories of Haleigh and Mariah and me just being silly will stay with me forever. In that playroom, I was temporarily removed from the sound of alarms and the fear of loss crushing my heart. Although I couldn't give Faith a normal life, I could provide Mariah and Haleigh some sense of normalcy.

Experiencing joy and peace during the worst time of my life was only possible by the grace of God. God asks me to follow him in all circumstances, even though I never know where he'll ask me to follow him next. God asked me to follow him into Faith's hospital room, but God also had me follow him into a playroom. In both rooms, God never left me.

Onesie One Day

"What if" scenarios started popping in my head: *What if Faith had been born on the third of May like she was supposed to be? What if I'd taken my wife to Strong Hospital instead of the other hospital the first time she began experiencing pain? What if our baby daughter dies? What if this is somehow my fault?*

One of the quickest ways to depression is to ask yourself "what if" questions. Attempting to shift my thinking, I leaned into hope. I imagined Faith wearing the onesie a friend had given her. I saw myself dressing her, putting her in her car seat, and bringing her home for the first time. I thought about laying her down in her crib at night. I figured that if I could believe Faith could grow healthy and strong, someday it would become possible.

During our time in the NICU, we began to transform Faith's hospital room into a child's room. We had children's books, small decorations, and colorful items on display everywhere, and we hung her first onesie above her isolette. I believed Faith's outfit of a diaper and hat, with accessories of tubes and wires, would someday be traded for that onesie. That onesie was not just a cute outfit, it was a symbol of hope.

The transformation of Faith's room was complete when my wife hung a giant pink poster board with black lettering that read: "God is within her, she will not fall; God will help her at break of day" (Psalm 46:5 [NIV]). This verse gave me hope and the confidence to see a better tomorrow for Faith. It was a great relief to see God's promises directed right at our family.

As I was reading the verse, nurses came rushing in. Faith's breathing was fading rapidly. Her oxygen had dropped dangerously low. I looked at the verse, then back at my daughter. God was telling me everything was going to be okay, but all I could see was everything that was not okay.

Every time Faith struggled to breathe, so did I. Each time she was in pain, my spirit was bruised. When Faith's heartbeat stopped, my heart raced in fear. I felt like we were in a constant tug-of-war. One of the world's scariest experiences is to place someone you love the most entirely in someone else's care. I often fail to trust things, people, and relationships with God because I doubt God's ability to do what is best. I knew God and the hospital staff had Faith's best interests at heart. I knew God existed and heard my prayers. I knew I had a relationship with God. But at that moment, I realized I was going to have to start believing him.

Motion Sickness

Suddenly, Faith's breathing regulated, but I could never forget we had a long road ahead. My stomach never settled, and I felt a lingering sense of grief with me each day. I felt like I was always on the verge of spilling my emotions onto everyone surrounding me. I would sleep for hours but never feel rested or relaxed. I was ready to give up.

I know everyone experiences ups and downs. But life cycles, crises and healing usually happen over months or years. My family's extreme ups and downs changed by the minute. We experienced bright highs followed by depressing lows multiple times each day. My physical body was neglected. My emotional state was being depleted, and my mental health was suffering.

I had to witness countless triggers of my daughter struggling to breathe. Have you ever watched someone you love die? Or have you ever watched someone you love die and come back to life multiple times? Each day I watched Faith die briefly, then witnessed her being brought back to life. I wondered how much more my daughter could take—and how much more I could take. The only thing I kept constant in my mind was the verse on that pink poster hanging above Faith.

Unexpressed Gratitude is Ingratitude

Faith's organs were beginning to shut down rapidly. Her ability to breathe was weakening. I knew she was dying, but my heart was not ready to accept it. I could not stomach the thought that she was exiting this world. I began to grasp the severity of the day when several nurses rushed into the room and asked my wife and me to step out so they could save Faith's life—again.

Desiré and I left the room, and fear began to cripple us. I thought to myself, *This is the end.* Faith's breathing stopped altogether. I began to sob uncontrollably. I sat down in a chair with my head dropped low and watched my tears bounce off my sneakers like a basketball. *These are the last moments of her life,* I thought. *This is our last day with her.* I pleaded with God for a miracle. I was a mess, and my daughter needed help. I tried to hope for a future for her that didn't include constant uncertainty and torment. I sat there motionless.

My heart was breaking as I heard the awful sound of the machine signaling that Faith had flatlined. Death was knocking at the door, and the hinges were coming off. While I was praying, a father from across the hallway came over to comfort me. He knelt on the floor so he could look me in the eye. Wiping the tears from my eyes, I attempted to look up, but my eyelids were too heavy with grief. I don't remember much of what he said, but one thing stuck out in my mind:

This gentleman was not a doctor, but he assured me my daughter would be taken care of and everything would be alright. Although I was filled with doubt, I chose to believe his words of encouragement to be true.

Suddenly, at the last possible moment, the nurses were able to revive her once again. I was relieved to know God was watching over Faith and was empowering the nurses to help my daughter live another moment. Celebrating the victory of this second chance, I thought about the compassionate father who had stopped to reach out to me during my lowest moment. I was humbled by how this man, whose son was fighting for his life, would take the time to be with me. I will never forget how he took the time to help me during the darkest moment of my life.

Before that father left for the day, he gave me a pink hat for Faith. His kindness began to thaw my frozen heart. I knew I was too emotionally exhausted to be everything my family needed me to be.

A few hours later, I had to go pick up the girls from school. I had to set aside my grieving father role to be a playful daddy for Haleigh and Mariah. I knew it wasn't fair to Haleigh and Mariah to see their dad an emotional mess all the time. I had to mask the very emotions that were shaping me.

The transition each day from hospital life to home life felt like a double life. In one world I was hoping to see Faith survive. In the other world I was hoping Haleigh and Mariah would thrive. I knew I had to be the best father for Faith, but I struggled to understand how to be a daddy to Mariah and Haleigh. I felt lost.

The next day, I thought to myself, *I need to thank the stranger who came to my aid during our crisis.* Arriving in the NICU, I searched the hall to find the father who had helped me. What I saw next horrified me.

Their room was empty. My heart sank and I began to weep, fearing the worst. When a room is empty in the NICU, it's usually because the child has "moved on." When I asked Desiré for an explanation, she confirmed my fears: The encourager who had helped me keep it together the day before had now lost his son. I was crushed. I'd missed the opportunity to thank him for all he had done.

I began to wonder why God spared my child but not his. God only knows. I was devastated for their family, who would have to learn how to move forward in life without their son. Losing someone you love is never easy. It's like trying to rebuild a new life, but with pieces missing.

I couldn't stop thinking about that man. Overwhelming pain is all I could feel for him. One of the world's greatest tragedies is to have all this love in your heart for another person and nowhere to express it. I shuddered thinking how he left the hospital without his son. He was living my biggest fear.

I felt guilt and grace at the same time. I had wanted to be there for him the same way he'd been there for me, and I'd missed the opportunity.

Minister and author Andy Stanley once said, "Unexpressed gratitude is ingratitude." This means if you don't tell someone thank you, what you're saying is, "I am not thankful for you. I don't need your help, and I could have done it without you."

Following that day, I have become more intentional about thanking others. I have not seen this man in person; however, I was able to thank him online two years later for all he did to give me hope when I felt hopeless. When I thought Faith was dying, a kind word of encouragement and compassion restored my hope.

FACING OUR FEARS

Weekdays Were Weak Days

Being home during the weekdays left me feeling weak. The isolation and loneliness reached new heights. Desiré and Faith were in the hospital, and I was home with the girls. After I put Haleigh and Mariah to bed at night, I felt nobody was there for me. What used to be a beautiful home started to feel like an empty house. I would sit alone in silence with all my thoughts. I could not sleep in our bed; it just did not feel right. I slept on the couch every night, burdened by loneliness. Trying to sleep through the chaos and feeling like the whole world did not understand me were some of my most brutal battles.

Spiritual Cheerleaders

Nothing else seems to matter when all you can think about is the one thing that scares you the most. As a parent, losing a child has always been my biggest fear. Now, this fearful possibility was becoming a probable reality with each passing day. Riding this merry-go-round of trauma was pushing me to the breaking point. Trying to get through this agony was leading to self-destruction. I was so blessed to have friends who would call me, text me, and pray for me every day.

Encouragement and support from friends gave me brief mental and emotional vacations. I remember one day getting a visit from one of my close friends. We spent the day worshipping and praying together. When we prepared to end our time together, we hugged. That hug sparked me to cry. I didn't just cry. I sobbed! At that moment, I didn't know how much more of this crisis I could handle. At that moment, I felt entirely accepted by him in all my grief. He didn't judge me for my crying and brokenness.

I can see quite a difference between spiritually healthy people and those who are in spiritual poverty. This is not because I consider myself a spiritual guru—I simply notice that people who place God as number one in their life are much more supportive of others than those who do not. Those who were spiritually healthy were a great support to our family. Individuals who didn't have a relationship with Jesus were not as able to be emotionally available.

I'm not saying that if you don't believe in Jesus, then you can't be a great support. In my experience, I am saying that those at peace with where they're going after they die can encourage another person facing mortality. When you don't know who or what you believe in, it's challenging to mentor another person in crisis—especially when that crisis combines a life-threatening illness with a spiritual battle.

You never know when you'll be the spark that sets someone's spirit on fire, providing light to the faint of heart.

Break Room

While sitting together in the NICU, Desiré and I were told that a social worker wanted to meet us. The topic of the conversation began to make me highly uncomfortable. All my emotions took off on a roller-coaster ride as soon as she said the word "arrangements." This nice word is a poor attempt to disguise how a person should prepare for the death of someone they love.

The word "arrangements"—so carefully chosen—didn't soften the blow; it infuriated me. The social worker was talking as if Faith's chance of survival was gone. This gut-wrenching conversation is one no parent should have, and I was not ready for it. The crisis of watching Faith die and be revived was bad enough, and now I had to talk about "arrangements" and prepare for how to move on after she was dead. I could imagine someone having this conversation with my children someday when I'm nearing the end of my life on earth, but not with me about my five-week-old infant. By the grace of God, I was able to sit through that discussion.

Understanding that this difficult conversation was supposed to help me, I reluctantly listened to the social worker ask questions about resuscitation and the desired protocol for nurses and doctors to make if her heart stopped beating again. I became sicker and sicker in my stomach. I thought to myself, *This can't be happening; this is not a real conversation about my daughter.*

As we ended our conversation, the anxiety chained me to the idea of death, and worry began to take center stage in my life.

Eye Need a Miracle

More than five weeks into Faith's life, I had not seen my daughter's eyes. Ever since her birth, her eyes had remained shut. Then one morning, while I was dropping Haleigh and Mariah off at school, my wife sent me a text saying Faith had opened her eyes. I held on to the words in that text as a sign Faith would be okay. I rushed back to the hospital to be a part of this miracle. When I arrived at the hospital, I was so excited to look into my daughter's eyes. Instead, her eyes were closed.

Despite my disappointment, I held on to hope she would open them again. I stared at Faith for hours with an expectation of being able to see each other eye-to-eye finally. Finally, her eyes broke the horizon of her eyelids. She looked directly into mine. Her gaze brought warmth to my heart and brightness to the room. As I looked into her eyes, she looked back at me as if to say, "Hi, Daddy, I see you." I smiled at her and said, "Hi, Faith." Our eyes were locked on each other in our first daddy-daughter staring contest. I refused to blink or look away until she closed her eyes, not knowing if I would ever see her beautiful eyes again.

Opening her eyes became a recurring gift to me. I was encouraged, even if opening her eyes was only a sign that she was 1 percent better. The slightest improvement was worth celebrating. In her hospital room that day, I'm not sure what was more unbelievable—Faith opening her eyes or my ability to smile joyfully.

We all can be a miracle. When we cannot get the miracle we are looking for, we can become a miracle for someone else. We become that miracle by choosing to love and choosing to heal. When we choose to be a miracle, we motivate those in despair to be repaired, by looking at each other with love, directly in the eye.

Divided Love

Trying to love while in a state of fear confused me. I knew I loved my daughter, Faith; I just was not sure how to love others. When I hugged Haleigh and Mariah, I thought of Faith. When I kissed my wife, I thought of Faith. My ability to love at the moment was gone. When I was with Desiré, Haleigh and Mariah physically, my attention was somewhere else. My heart and mind constantly wandered back to Faith's hospital room. I felt like I had a shattered heart; no matter where I went, a part of me was never with me. Nothing was the same.

I began to spend more and more time thinking about Faith's future. I wondered who she would grow to look like. I wondered whose personality she would have. I imagined whose laugh she would have—her mom's or mine. I hoped neither because we both have some obnoxious laughs. I considered which sister she would take after more. I wondered if she would be healed. When could we bring her home? More and more, I found myself trying to put our family puzzle together with Faith in the middle of it all. With my thoughts racing, my body began to slow down. I was exhausted trying to live life at two different speeds.

Time kept moving and I could not stop it. The sound of a ticking clock was enough to cause a panic attack. It was sobering to realize that Faith's life and mine were made up of the ticks of a clock. I struggled to understand why it appeared as if the second-hand for my life slowed down, and Faith's seemed to speed up. I sensed her time was running out.

Unshakeable Faith

One day while I was picking up Mariah from school, there seemed to be an air of tension as soon as I entered the classroom. The entire mood shifted from one of laughter to one of pity. We lived in a small town where everyone knows everything about everyone, so it was no secret our daughter was fighting for her life. I could feel people looking at me differently. People tried to be encouraging and wanted to know how she was doing. In that moment, I felt like I'd become only the dad deeply struggling with a child on the verge of death. I'd been labeled "poor Jesse," because when they saw me, they saw death. I was hoping that instead they would see faith.

People zoomed in on my life as if it was some reality TV show. I knew I was being watched closer than ever before, especially by those who did not believe in God. I was aware that others were now placing me under a microscope, to see if this God thing was for real. I knew my actions might be the only Bible some people would ever read. People wanted proof and evidence that God was real. I decided I would do my best to become the confirmation of the God they were searching for. I understood that this crisis was my opportunity to show Christ to others.

Life seemed to be poking and prodding at me until I would lash out at others. If the saying "hurting people hurt people" is true, it was only a matter of time before I would hurt someone deeply. I felt as if my spirit was bending and bending, and I was going to snap. The recurring trauma of the hospital room each day felt like suffocation. Then I would catch my breath, only to start suffocating again. I felt like I was only one heartbeat away from losing my sanity and my life.

I was desperate for Faith's healing and my own. I also recognized I was not alone; it seems everyone is desperate for some type of healing. Everyone is hurting in some way. My wounds just happened to be more public. It was no secret I was a mess, but I wanted God to use my mess as a message of hope for others. If there had ever been a time to be a living and loving example of God, I knew this was the time. Being able to show that God is good even when life does not feel good became my mission. Whether Faith lived or died, I knew that I would make sure Faith's life would touch others for the rest of my life.

I learned something I believe that might be true for all of us: The deeper my scars, the wider my reach. My pain is a guide to my purpose and a direction for the wounded to follow.

God Will Give You More than You Can Handle

While shaving one morning, I decided to listen to some music. My hope was that the music would give me the emotional and mental vacation I needed. Then a random song came on, and suddenly I became an emotional wreck. The song, which is about losing someone you love, triggered something buried deep inside me. In trying to be "strong," I had hidden my feelings, to appear manly. As the song played, the perfectly built wall failed as I wept uncontrollably. I hid in the bathroom while trying to rebuild the wall and re-hide my emotions. I stayed in the bathroom until I could calm myself down and wipe away any evidence of tears.

I have been burying my emotions my entire life. Like most men, I tend to walk around like everything is alright, even when deep down everything is messy. I wasn't comfortable letting my family see me as an emotional mess. I have always felt like I must be the strong one. I kept thinking I needed to hold it together, even though I had lost my grip. I was coming to grips with the idea that refusing to show any emotions is more cowardly than brave.

As the leader of the family, I was not feeling like a leader. I would look at Desiré, Haleigh and Mariah and wonder how they were coping. I knew I was headed on a downward spiral as I continued to put on the mask of masculinity. I moved forward based on how I'd been taught men should act, pretending everything was fine and following the code of "suck it up and keep on keeping on." I was too broken to keep the family together the way I should have, and I felt like a failure. Being so riddled with fear, I thought there was no way I could be a great example of a family man.

As these fearful thoughts raced through my mind, a phrase I thought was from the Bible began to echo in my head: "God won't ever give you more than you can handle." This sounded like one of the biggest lies I'd ever heard.

As the pain was suffocating me, I reached out to God to renew my shattered spirit. It seemed that every time I forgot about God, my pain became unbearable.

When I took the time to look up the entire verse, I learned it says, "You are tempted in the same way all other human beings are. God is faithful. He will not let you be tempted any more than you can take. But when you are tempted, God will give you a way out. Then you will be able to deal with it" (1 Corinthians 10:13[NIRV]). If we refuse to include God, life's tragedies will be more than we can handle. When we invite God into our lives, nothing that happens to us is more than we can take. It is God's help that gets us through, not simply our drive and determination.

I began to wonder if everything was perfect, would I need to cry out for God? If all life's circumstances were ideal, my need and dependence on God would cease to exist. I would be functioning on my strength, desire and willpower. All those things are great to have, but they have limitations. All the horrendous injustices and cruel suffering in the world point me towards the need for God. For a perfect world to exist, we would all have to be puppets, with no free will and no choice so that we could never choose evil. But that's no way to live. God loves us enough to let us choose.

In raising my girls, I have learned the importance of allowing them to make choices. As they get older and learn more about making bigger choices, I will give them more opportunities to do so. There will come a time when they will be adults and get to make all of their choices on their own. Hopefully by then I will have shown them the path they should take, but the choice of whether to follow it is ultimately theirs. I would love it if they would follow all my instructions for life, but I certainly will not force them. I love them enough to let them choose.

Even if I could be the greatest dad, I will never be able to protect my daughters from everything. Life will happen, and I will be there for them as long as God allows me to be. My inability to protect them from everything does do not make me less of a dad. Dads can be huge burdens or tremendous blessings to their kids. Still, no dad can compare to our heavenly Father.

It is interesting how one random song caused all these thoughts to flow through my head. That song, "How Could You Leave Us," by NF, unlocked the pain I was denying. As I refocused on getting ready for the hospital visit, I paused to remind myself of all the blessings from the past. I knew God had never failed me and he would not forget me now. My pain and Faith's suffering did not stop because I believed in God. However, I was able to catch glimpses of his love and grace during this painful time. God never said, "Jesse, you will not have pain," but he did promise I will never have to walk through the pain alone. I know that following God is not an insurance policy from the storms of life, but it is protection from drowning while I am in them. Life will occasionally give me more than I can handle on my own, but I know it can't ever give me more than God can handle.

Musical Healing

I was inspired watching Desiré making sure Faith was getting the best care. While we were with Faith in her NICU room we would play worship music. When one of the nurses was caring for our daughter, she asked my wife, "What is this music you're listening to?" Desiré said it was one of the more popular songs in Christian music. Something about this song made the nurse talk about her struggle with her loss. She told Desiré that her father had recently died, and she had found the music comforting. She said the song gave her hope, and she asked for some additional radio stations where she could find more songs like it. My wife told her about the radio station KLOVE and other artists and songs to listen to. It was remarkable to me that during the worst time of her entire life, Desiré was still encouraging another person and showing love and compassion.

In a world where pain brings war, in God's plan, pain brings peace and unity. We get to choose what to do with the suffering and unfair circumstances of our life. We decide to let them either divide us or unite us. Many of us carry heavy burdens that would be much lighter if we simply share the load with someone else.

It amazes me to see how suffering can turn into healing through the power of worship music. By remaining open-minded to the existence and presence of God, we increase our chances of healing. Being an overcomer is about choosing how you will heal. Some people attempt to "heal" with vengeance and bitterness. Other people heal with patience and grace. In these painful moments, my wife and I turn to worship music.

Most of the time, the suffering we experience is meant not only to teach us how to cope, but, more importantly, to teach others how to hope. As John Acuff says, "There's no hope without hurt." Hurt is a prerequisite to experiencing hope. We all need to help others recover, especially if we have experienced tremendous grief. If you keep the suffering to yourself, you suffer more. If you help others with their suffering, they can begin healing, and so can you. Grief is not just a burden—it provides wisdom and empowerment. I believe that, somewhere, someone is depending on you to share your pain with them. People need to see real life examples of people going from tragedy to triumph. Your pain can be an answered prayer to someone else's recovery. When you look at suffering through the eyes of opportunity, it is an honor to suffer for a season, because it can lead to helping someone else heal for a lifetime.

A Fool for a Cause

My wife and I had grand plans for Faith, but what we planned and what might happen were feeling like two different things. In February, the days were much colder. And for a moment I selfishly thought of my birthday, thinking, *This year the perfect gift would be for Faith to be healed.* Despite the challenging circumstances, my wife still wanted to do something for my birthday.

Desiré's birthday gift was to sign me up for a Polar Plunge! She has a fantastic sense of humor. The Polar Plunge is where insane people agree to go into freezing water during the coldest time of the year to raise money for the Special Olympics. I thought to myself, *There must be a warmer way to raise money.* When Desiré told me the plan, I laughed and reluctantly agreed to be a fool for a good cause.

Insane ideas are best shared, so I recruited a couple of friends to join me for the plunge. Being in an uncomfortable situation is more tolerable when someone joins me in the discomfort. I realized I couldn't afford to indulge in unhealthy habits and decided to use this Polar Plunge as an opportunity to grow. Doing something completely out of my comfort zone would give me the confidence to take on future challenges.

I finally made it to the Polar Plunge tent area to do one of the craziest things of my entire life. As plunge time approached, I began looking at the snowy, ice-covered lake. The rush of energy was like nothing I had experienced before. My courage began to grow, even though I was wearing only sweatpants on this cold winter day. It was 30 degrees outside, and I was about to go swimming just to prove I was man enough. Desiré has called me a complete pansy more than once, because when I'm cold, I complain like a baby with a wet diaper. Truthfully, I think she challenged me to do this for two reasons: first, to watch me cry and whine from the severe cold, and second, because she knew we both needed something to shock us back into life. And Desiré knows how to get her point across.

When it came time to approach the lake, I attempted to put my feet in the water like every other sane person did that day. Then suddenly, my friend tackled me, and I was fully submerged in Lake Ontario in February. To my surprise, I did not feel the cold water. For the moment, I was not cold. However, as soon as I stepped out of the water, the adrenaline wore off and cold crashed into my body like a truckful of reality. My feet felt like someone was hitting them with the claw side of a hammer as I raced to the warming hut.

The short walk from the ice-cold water to the heated building felt like an eternity. To my surprise, I managed to survive, as I thought to myself, *I am such a fool.* I had bruises from the ice smashing against my body. Then I thought about how great it was to be part of something like this to benefit those in need.

I learned that it's essential to take a baby step outside of my comfort zone and put both feet into a new adventure. Sometimes, however, we need someone to tackle us and help us face what is too difficult to handle on our own.

As fun as the Polar Plunge was, it soon was time to head back to the hospital and be with Faith. As Desiré and I were leaving, I asked my friend who had plunged with me why he'd decided to be a complete fool and jump in the freezing water too. He answered, "Because I wanted to honor your daughter." His answer is something I will never forget. His act of compassion toward my daughter, whom he had never met, spoke volumes about his character. Although we were miles away from the hospital, Faith's presence was with me.

Just Pray

While watching my daughter struggle to breathe, I became more and more aware of how much every one of us needs God's help, even just to breathe. As I became more aware of God's presence in my life, I could see there has never been a moment where God has left me. I always have access to the most extraordinary power globally, and in the past, I have chosen not to accept it. During the times when my ability becomes limited, I need to become aware of God's voice. I often think I have things under control or God does not exist or care. It is then that I need to take a time-out and plug back into the power source of love and life.

Sometimes bad things happen to "good" people. Sometimes good things happen to "bad" people. Either way, neither case disproves the existence of God. Pain is meant to reveal our need for healing through God. Watching Faith suffer in her isolette did not negate the presence of God. It did deepen my need for God to help me get through the suffering.

February 14 arrived, and Faith's health took a turn for the worst. She was moved to a new monitor because of her deteriorating health. I could see her body starting to swell and turning pale. More doctors and nurses were monitoring her. As each hour passed, an entire team of nurses and doctors lined up outside the NICU, waiting for Faith's next flatline to appear. The possibility of Faith dying was at an all-time high. We knew her organs were failing, and her chance of survival was slipping away.

During all this, a priest came into Faith's room and asked Desiré and me about our spiritual beliefs and if he could do anything to support our family. Mid-conversation with the priest, my wife received a family member's message that they had just lost their father. As she interrupted the conversation to help our grieving family member, Desiré said something I will never forget. She said to the priest, "Someone needs prayer more than we do. Could you please pray for our loved one who just lost his father?" I thought the priest was going to fall over from shock. He seemed not to understand how a mother who might lose her child at any moment would ask for prayer for someone else, yet he agreed.

During our stay in the NICU, a mom invited her entire family to come and visit their baby before she died. Watching the woman struggle as she explained over and over why she wanted everyone to visit one last time, Desiré went up to her and grabbed her hands and began praying right there in front of everyone. As Desiré prayed with her, they both began to cry. As I stood there watching them pray together, I sensed God's peace. I was also blessed to know that my children got to see their mom publicly declare her faith in God.

FAITH TAKES FLIGHT

Eagle Aloft

When February 15 arrived, the fear for Faith's life became more real with each passing hour. Desiré's mom came with me to the hospital. While I was driving and talking to her about Faith and the girls, suddenly, a huge, beautiful bald eagle soared past the car. As I watched the eagle fly upwards, I felt something come over me. I have seen eagles in flight countless times in my life, but this experience was something profoundly different. In my mind I heard, "But those who hope in the Lord will renew their strength. They will soar on wings like eagles; they will run and not grow weary, they will walk and not be faint" (Isaiah 40:31). In my spirit, I knew that God was reminding me not to grow weary but to lean on him. Up until this moment I had been running on emotional and spiritual fumes. With all the pain my daughter was dealing with and all the heartache I felt was soon approaching, it was clear God was telling me to find rest in him.

As I continued to drive and think about the eagle, another Scripture came to mind, Deuteronomy 32:11: "Like an eagle that stirs up its nest and hovers over its young, that spreads its wings to catch them and carries them aloft." The eagle hovering over me was a sign to prepare me for the support I would need. The hovering also let me know God was hovering over Faith.

Aloft was a word I didn't completely understand, so I did a little research. I learned that aloft means "into the sky, up high and heavenward." Without God saying the words directly, He was telling me Faith would be going upward soon. Faith's time on earth was quickly fading. I knew that, when she left this earth, she was going heavenward.

God will use anything to show me He cares. My starting point to learn about God's plan is often through Scripture and prayer. Other times, it's revealed through relationships and situations. Sometimes it's even in a road sign, a song, a diagnosis, or an eagle.

What current circumstance in your life has your attention? God knows you and knows what can get your attention. Maybe it's not an eagle, but something else. The randomness of life is not always random if you take a moment to reflect. He might be using some circumstances, or someone, to try to get you to move closer to him. The signs are not always obvious, prominent, or consistent; however, God will strategically show you a revelation in a creative way that speaks to you. You just need to have enough faith and hope to spread your wings, and he will catch you and bring you aloft.

Blessings?

Twenty minutes after I left the hospital to take my mother-in-law back home, my phone began to ring. Seeing Desiré's name appear on the phone made my heart sink to the pit of my stomach. I could sense something was wrong. When I answered, it became clear that she was more concerned than ever before. Desiré told me to come back to the hospital as quickly as possible after dropping her mother off. As I listened to Desiré, I was emotionally drained and didn't think

I could take another second of just waiting in the NICU. I told Desiré I would be there as quickly as I could, and then said goodbye.

Arriving at the hospital, I was consumed with fear. Desiré knew that Faith's health was declining rapidly, and it could be a matter of hours or minutes before she flatlined for the final time. Desiré looked at the nurse and said, "She's dying!" The nurse looked slowly at Faith and silently agreed. Although I knew my wife and the nurse understood more than I did about Faith's condition, I could not accept that Faith was dying.

After dropping Desiré's mother off and returning to the hospital I joined Desiré at Faith's side. The following morning it was clear that Faith's body had been shutting down for the past eight hours, we both were exhausted. Desiré had not slept in days, and stress took over, so it became my job to stand watch over Faith.

As I sat there watching Faith, time seemed to slow down. I wondered how God was going to heal her. I began to play some music, hoping to find some comfort. I choose to loop the song "Blessings" by Lecrae, then sat back to listen and try to breathe. The lyrics include the lines "Every loss is a lesson" and "I'm too busy counting all these blessings." As music filled the room, I began to feel God prompting me to turn the music off and just be with Faith in silence for a moment. I turned off the music and stared at my daughter harder than ever before. God wanted me to count this blessing of spending these precious seconds on earth together, alone.

My stomach began to turn. I knew that this was going to be Faith's last day on earth. I looked over at my wife, who had finally fallen asleep.

Somewhere, I had heard that people in hospice care keep fighting until they have made peace with their loved ones. Desiré had given her grandmother's rosary beads to Faith as a going-away and welcome-home gift all rolled into one. Desiré and Faith had made peace with each other, and now it was my turn.

For Faith to be entirely free to join her heavenly father, she needed me to make peace with her leaving. Faith needed me to let her go. I was in great pain that she was leaving me, but I was also grateful she could spend these last moments with just me. As I smiled at her one last time, all of Faith's levels dropped—she was flatlining.

Suddenly, Desiré woke up to the sound of buzzers and alarms signaling Faith's life was coming to an end. One more time, the doctor and nurses came into the room and attempted to save Faith, but it was too late. Faith was leaving us. Desiré and I sobbed uncontrollably as I hugged Desiré tighter than ever before.

Standing next to my dying baby daughter, I began to question how God could consider this a blessing. Yes, spending the last few moments on earth with my daughter did bring me some peace, but I could not call it a blessing. I am not sure what to call it. The pain of spending those last seconds of her life was unbearable. She was placed in our arms, and we held Faith together, for the first and last time.

Dying to Live

Together we prayed and asked God to take care of our daughter, and to save a place for her in heaven alongside him. Tears of despair mixed with tears of hope ran down my face. Desiré slowly rocked Faith to sleep for the final time. We sat together and told Faith how much we loved her and how much she meant to us. We reminded her about the great Father who is waiting for her.

In those final moments, Desiré, Faith, God and I all had a heart-to-heart conversation, and then we said goodbye to Faith. In the most challenging moment of my life, I felt God's presence welcoming her home.

Losing Custody

Looking back, it is sobering to think the worst day of my entire life was the best day of Faith's. On that day, Faith was released from pain and struggle and welcomed into heaven.

By far the most challenging thing for any parent to do is to release their children into the care and custody of someone else. I had been in a custody battle before, but this custody battle with God over Faith was unlike any other. There was no opportunity to negotiate co-parenting or any fifty-fifty split. There would be no holiday sharing. No switching on birthdays. No weekend visitation. No judge could undo the decision of death. A permanent eternal custody order has been decided. We had lost custody of Faith to God.

At the moment of Faith's death, the spiritual presence of God was so forceful, I felt as if the walls of the room were expanding outward and would burst from trying to hold his massive presence. God's breath filled the room. With Faith's last breath, God breathed her into heaven. A loud ringing sound penetrated my ears. I knew the exact moment her spirit was released.

Everything happened just as I had read in Psalm 46:5: "God is within her, she will not fall; God will help her at break of day." Often, I think the promises of Scripture are meant for what happens for us here on earth. And yet much of Scripture is meant for what happens in the next life. At the break of day, God did not let Faith fall. God took Faith aloft. God helped Faith just as He said he would. God's healing was complete. On that cold morning of February 16, 2017, Faith was healed. God answered my prayer. I knew deep down my Faith was rescued at the break of day.

42 Days

As I held on to Faith's lifeless body, I became exhausted from grief. I could have raged against the doctors and cursed them for everything that had happened over the previous forty-two days. Instead, as a doctor knelt beside me searching for words, I lifted my eyes and said, "Thank you." I thanked him for his commitment and dedication to trying to heal Faith.

The doctor looked back and reminded me of the forty-two days Faith and I had shared. He wanted me to cherish those forty-two days. She and I had forty-two days of memories I could carry with me for the rest of my life. I found comfort in his words. Oddly, I am thankful it was forty-two days instead of four years or ten years or fifteen years. I'm not saying that losing a child as an infant is not the hardest thing in the world. But if we'd brought Faith home and she'd lived a few years before dying from complications of a premature birth, that loss would have been even harder.

I found comfort knowing Faith was no longer suffering and was living in perfect peace and joy. I had a huge hole in my heart, which I knew would be there until I saw her again, but I found comfort in the promise of heaven.

I placed Faith's lifeless body back into her bed. It was time to leave Faith and this room forever. As we made our way out of the NICU, I stopped and turned around, hoping everything that had just happened was a terrible nightmare.

Nothing changed. She was gone; I was awake. I let out an excruciating scream and stumbled out of the NICU. I had to accept that my daughter was gone.

Heart-Breaking News

Leaving the hospital for the final time, Desiré and I went to the Ronald McDonald House. The emotional roller coaster of the previous forty-two days came crashing in on us. Going to sleep and waking up without Faith in our lives was not going to be easy, but at that moment we both just needed silence and each other. We went into the bedroom and laid there in tears, eventually crying ourselves to sleep.

That night was the longest night of my entire life. I tossed and turned, trying to understand what life would look like next. Desiré and I seemed to be in sync about the challenges ahead. As I started my morning, I realized that I was not in a bad dream. The reality was that my daughter Faith was dead.

Desiré and I packed and said goodbye to the staff at the Ronald McDonald House. We would be leaving with no diaper bag to carry. No car seat to load. No baby to hold. Just grief.

We began the torturous drive home. We knew Haleigh would be there wanting to know how her baby sister was doing. We were terrified at the thought of breaking the news to Haleigh that Faith was dead, because it meant breaking her heart.

I have read many parenting books over the years, and none of them ever explained how to tell your child one of their siblings has died. As I drove in a daze, I struggled to understand how to break such painful news to Haleigh with a shattered spirit. As we got closer to home, Desiré and I briefly discussed how we would handle that conversation. Heading for the door, we were both nervous, exhausted and trembling about what would happen when we stepped inside the house. The most devastating moment of Haleigh's life was about to happen.

Haleigh Hurts

Haleigh was the first person we talked to about Faith's death. Soon we would leave a trail of broken hearts among our loved ones with the same news. We asked Haleigh to sit down, hoping to make her comfortable. Desiré and I looked at each other, our body language communicating the question, "Who's going to tell her?" The awkward silence became dreadful. We needed to tell Haleigh, but we didn't know how to start. Being direct and truthful with Haleigh was the best thing for her at that moment. Finally, Desiré spoke.

She sat Haleigh on her lap and told her that Faith was gone and no longer in pain. Haleigh erupted into tears. Her tears caused our tears to flow. My wound of loss was ripped open even wider. Haleigh's sobbing was unlike anything I'd ever heard from her before—it came from a deep place of despair and it broke me entirely.

All I'd wanted to do was protect Haleigh and Mariah during the previous forty-two days, but I could protect them no longer. I felt like I'd failed as a father. The feeling of not being able to heal the pain brought me to a new low point. Haleigh's tears have never been so deep and had never been so violent. Our hugs had never been so tight as they were at that moment.

Haleigh was hurting, and I only wanted to help her hurt a little less. I wanted the hurt to vanish, but it only continued to spread. I remember thinking to myself, *If I'm going to be constantly on the verge of a breakdown, how will Haleigh handle Faith's death?*

We sat there holding each other and crying and grieving for what felt like an eternity. Sharing the news of Faith's death with my ten-year-old daughter punctured a deep hole in my heart. After the sobbing eased, we then had to plan how we would share the news with Mariah.

Mariah's Turn

The silence that followed our conversation with Haleigh was deafening. The clock still ticked, the earth still spun, and our hearts kept beating, but life seemed to stop. Watching Desiré dump out saved breast milk was just another reminder that my dreams for Faith were going down the drain.

Mariah was in Philadelphia visiting her mother. I knew I needed to call her mother and tell her that we needed to pick up Mariah a few days early, but I wanted just to hide instead.

Desiré and I talked about telling Mariah, hoping to find a better way of handling things than we had with Haleigh. We knew we had to be the ones to tell Mariah, and that it would crush her spirit. She had cared so much for her younger sister. Before picking up Mariah, we decided that telling her in the car while driving home from Philadelphia was not the best option. So, we stopped at Dunkin Donuts to have lunch and talk.

After we ordered, we went outside and sat down in silence. Desiré and I looked at each other again, wondering who was going to tell Mariah. I did not want to tell her that her two-year-long prayer of having a younger sister had been answered with a heart-breaking "No." As I began to tell her about Faith, I stumbled over my words.

Mariah could sense something was wrong, and after stuttering around, I blurted out, "Faith is in heaven."

At that moment I felt as if time froze. Desiré and I waited for Mariah's reaction. Our extremely talkative child was silent. After a pause, which felt like forever, Mariah said, "Let's go." Mariah picked up her meal and walked to the car. We followed her lead. Mariah did not speak or show any emotion as she got back into the car. She became a statue of emptiness. The feeling of nothingness was everywhere.

Together in silence we continued our drive home. Every few seconds I would glance in the mirror to see how Mariah was doing. It was clear that Mariah was in shock. Mariah's expression changed to a look of anger mixed with sorrow. Glaring heavenward, it appeared as if she was scolding God. Mariah clearly was wrestling with God and her faith. Suddenly, Mariah burst into tears and began wailing uncontrollably.

As I drove on, Desiré crawled into the back seat to hold Mariah as she continued to scream and rage over the loss of her baby sister. Her screams drowned out the city traffic, her tears streamed down, and her heart was shattering into pieces. Tears rolled down my face as I watched another heartbreak. *What is happening to my family? What am I doing to them? How will we survive?* These were my thoughts as we drove for the next five hours.

That long drive was not enough time to heal. I imagined it would probably take years to heal, and maybe a lifetime to understand what was happening. I wanted to find peace so I could show my family that peace could be found. I held on to the hope that God could make us whole again.

Being together as a family was both encouraging and devastating. Encouraging because I love being with my family and being a dad and a husband, but devasting because of Faith's absence.

Simple things brought up painful reminders. Setting the table with four plates instead of five was a reminder that there was an open space at the table with no one to fill it. In these moments, feelings of grief and guilt would bring on crippling panic attacks.

Arrangements

Desiré and I had agreed that we did not want any attention. What we wanted most was just to crawl under a rock and hide. So, when I sat with the funeral director discussing the cremation of Faith's body, her death became more real to me than ever before. Sitting alone at the funeral home, I had to flip through page after page of urns, trying to decide on the perfect option for Faith. Eventually I found a beautiful blue urn with butterflies; it seemed like something Faith would have wanted.

You can't heal in the same environment that wounded you.

-Toby Mac

As the funeral home-made preparations for Faith service, Desiré told me she needed to get away from everything. She needed to go as far away as she could from all the reminders and memories of the last few weeks. We settled on a trip to California. We wanted sunshine, we wanted warmth, and we needed to feel life again. The trip would also offer an escape from the countless people continuously asking us how Faith was doing.

Desiré and I called some family members to tell them about Faith's passing. We received a wide range of reactions, from silence and empathy to exploding rage. We were so emotionally exhausted that we finally decided to stop telling any more people, and just focus on us and our escape.

As we traveled to California, I reflected on one phone call from my best friend, whom I love like a brother. When I told him that Faith had died, he became emotional. I just needed to know someone cared. I needed to know I was not alone. He shared in my suffering. I didn't need any words. I just needed someone to cry with me.

NO ESCAPE

Mountain Valley God

Even though Desiré was in pain from her surgery, she was determined that we would hike Ryan Mountain as a family. Desiré's perseverance and her ability to push through her physical and emotional pain inspired each of us to reach the summit that day.

Climbing Ryan Mountain together was our way of healing after going through such a tragic loss. Ryan Mountain was symbolic of our life and our struggles. Many times, each of us wanted to quit, but we each needed to find a way to push through to reach the summit.

When we reached the summit, we took a family photo—the first without Faith. Looking at the photo caused me to focus on what was missing instead of appreciating the moment. Although outwardly I was cheering for our family, internally I was once again grieving for life moving forward without Faith.

I learned that the journey of completing anything of significance requires setbacks and discomfort. No one reaches the summit of success accidentally. No one can randomly land on the top of a mountain. Whether I feel on top of the world or in the deepest valley, God uses both to draw me closer to him. As painful as the valley is and as beautiful as the mountain top is, both are equally necessary for my growth. Although I enjoy the mountain tops more, my awareness of God has been clearer in the valleys.

Get Help

California gave us a break, but not an escape. When we got home, we had to face what we had temporarily run away from. We came home to flowers and sympathy cards. Every petal was appreciated, and every card was cherished. Still, our house felt empty.

Desiré and I decided we needed to sign up for Steppingstone. Steppingstone is a support group that allowed our daughters to process their loss with other children who also were dealing with a loved one's death. This program also allowed Desiré and me to connect with other adults who had suffered loss. In addition to Steppingstone, we joined a grief group through our church. Both groups provided great relationships where we could process the loss of Faith.

Most of the breakthroughs in my life seem to require some sort of emotional explosion. I have found when tears break out, a breakthrough comes next. If you have suffered a loss, get help immediately. If you know anyone who has suffered a loss recently, help them get the help they need. Grieving is more manageable when it is done in community.

When people experience a traumatic event, I read somewhere that they subconsciously become stuck at the age the crisis happened. For me, I became frozen at the age of thirty, the time of Faith's death.

When you outlive your spouse, you become a widow or widower. When children lose their parents, they are orphans. But, just as there is no name for a mom or a dad who has lost a child, no word could define the pain I carry from losing my daughter. Not having a word to define what I felt caused even more confusion and anguish.

If you're experiencing pain that seems unbearable and feel like ending it all, there is a number you can call—the National Suicide Prevention Lifeline is available to help you 24/7, at 1-800-273-8255.

Traumatic Healing

Suffering a loss is painful but having to relive the loss daily is excruciating. After talking with family and close friends, we had hoped that the news of Faith's death would be told to everyone else. This did not turn out to be the case. Sharing the news began to feel like a daily responsibility. Leaving the house to go to school, work, or even the grocery store gave me anxiety. I desperately wanted to avoid anyone asking me, "How is your daughter doing?" I knew I couldn't be angry with anyone for not knowing, but I grew tired of trying to figure out the polite way to answer that question.

Each conversation about Faith's death triggered a ruthless flashback to that moment of watching her take her last breath. Each conversation caused my stomach to turn like old milk. I became sick from having to answer the worst question I'd ever heard. When people first asked about Faith, I would do my best to collect myself, keep a poker face, and answer calmly, "She's no longer with us; she passed away." But those interactions exhausted me, so I would move on before they could ask for any details or offer any false hope.

I soon realized I had been answering their question incorrectly. When people asked how my daughter was doing, I had been giving a negative response, answering how *I* was doing, and not Faith. I was a mess, stressed and downright depressed. As uncomfortable as each conversation was, the awkwardness began to lead to restoration. The pain of recounting Faith's death kept mounting. I needed some way to release everything that was bottled up inside of me. I no longer wanted to tell half the story. I needed to open up and confess that I was living in great pain.

By selfishly focusing on my feelings about Faith's death, I minimized what God had done. I had once believed that suffering happened because God was absent. Yet, my time in Faith's hospital room taught me that God's presence was more present in suffering than in my victories. I could not separate where my loss ended and where Faith's healing began. Faith's death became linked to my identity, which was draining the life out of me. If I could shift my perspective from Faith's death on earth to what happened *after* her death, I could begin to heal.

By choosing to heal, I was able to answer differently the question about how Faith was doing. God was using that hard question to cause me to grow stronger and face reality I was attempting to deny.

Finally, when people asked how Faith was doing, I could look them in the eye with assurance and confidence and answer, "Faith is doing great; she is in heaven now." I was learning that where my strength ended, God's strength in me began. It amazed me that I'd come to the point that I could answer this question without a complete meltdown. I no longer suffered from such intense grief that I felt like I needed to hide. Day by day, God was setting me free by teaching me to no longer be a prisoner to the past.

Destruction to Restoration

I used to think relapses only pertained to people who were addicted to drugs. Through the grieving process, I learned that I was not immune to the relapse of grief. I felt abandoned, and even developed an obsession with my grief. I would find myself falling into depression, and experience traumatic NICU flashbacks.

I was in a dark place. Thinking my life without Faith did not have purpose or value, I dreaded the thought of continuing to breathe each day. I felt that I needed to see Faith at any cost. I knew she could not see me, so I fantasized about how I could see Faith again.

I thought, *If I can't be her daddy on earth, let me be her daddy in heaven.* As I drove to work, I thought, *If I get into a car accident, I can leave my brokenness behind and be complete with Faith.* I wanted to die, to end my suffering. A car accident would be perfect because my wife and children would think I had died accidentally. Sadly, committing suicide felt like the only way to escape this pain.

Every time I considered suicide, something would hold me back. I prayed something terrible would happen to me. I pleaded again and again for God to take my life, as earnestly as I'd prayed to God to keep Faith alive. Every morning I would wake up crying because I was still alive. When I went to sleep, I wanted to stay asleep forever.

I also knew that, if I died, I would leave my family more broken than ever. When I looked at Desiré, Haleigh and Mariah, I realized I could never leave them. They needed me, and I needed them. My love for the rest of my family was unfinished. My life needed a purpose, even when I wasn't sure what that purpose was.

Although I no longer prayed for death, life was far from normal. Despite my pain and trauma, I vowed to rededicate myself to being the best possible father to Haleigh and Mariah. Being a dad always came naturally to me, but being a husband was something I always struggled to be. Feeling emotionally depleted, I decided to isolate myself from my wife and focus on making more good memories with Haleigh and Mariah. Moving from my addiction to grief to my addiction to being a perfect dad, I began to idolize and worship our children. They became my sole purpose. The fear of losing one of them became so overwhelming that I became consumed with watching everything they did, every moment of every day.

My grief over Faith threatened my marriage. My failure to choose to heal our marriage wounded my wife. Desiré and I began to argue constantly, and I withdrew from our relationship. I became verbally abusive, and our communication became toxic. I pushed her away to the point that she was about to leave me. I was failing as a husband and I had become an overbearing dad.

Desiré somehow saw a way for our marriage to be restored. She did not give up when she could have. Her refusal to quit on me and our marriage gave us the opportunity for restoration. Desiré chose to love me when I was unlovable. This was a great example of how Jesus loves.

Desiré and I had lost our daughter Faith, but if we lost our marriage and our faith in God, we would have lost everything. Desiré decided she was not going to lose her faith or her marriage.

During that time, God was restoring our faith and rebuilding our shattered hearts and our marriage. Desiré and I still struggle like everyone else, but we never give up. We keep the faith.

MOVING FORWARD

Vacation with Strangers

A month after our return from California, a couple that we only knew casually from church approached us about a vacation they were planning. They were strangers and they invited us to go on vacation with them. They had rented a beach house and had space for another family to join them. To make the invitation even more interesting, another family was going who were strangers to us. The idea of a week-long vacation in the same house with two families we barely knew sounded insane, but, heck, it was a week at the beach!

Something told me I should accept their offer. Desiré and I decided this would be a great way to get to know some new people and make new friends. The surprising part about this adventure was that we were not nervous or concerned. We felt God was shifting our relationships, and this beach trip was the beginning of that shift and lifelong friendships. Everyone is invited to something great and unique or even odd at some point in life. If they have faith to step out, God can do amazing things.

Desiré and I were encouraged by the other families during this vacation, and recognized they were the type of people we needed to do life with. We became intentional about surrounding ourselves with more kind, generous, encouraging, and trustworthy people, no matter how awkward it might be at first.

Being in the company of these faith-filled, positive people caused me to realize I needed to remove a few toxic people from my life. I wanted to surround myself with people who focused on healthy relationships. The man who invited us is now one of my closest friends. He is someone I admire, respect and love like a big brother. He pushes me to grow in my faith and become a more dedicated husband, father, and leader for my family.

I am always amazed how the smallest acts that are done with great love can change the lives of others. The next time you see a person or family hurting, my advice is just to step out in faith and do something to help. Make them dinner, take them out to dinner, invite them to your house, just be kind. There are countless kind gestures you can do to make someone's pain a little less painful. No matter how weird it might seem, just be there. You never know how much impact you can have on someone or how a lifelong relationship can be formed from one generous gesture. Reach out, make the invitation, accept the invitation, or just go on a vacation with strangers.

How Are You in School Right Now?

Just when I felt I had things in control and was moving forward in my recovery, I stumbled upon a document from the hospital I had not seen before. As I looked at an envelope with Faith's name, I was compelled to open it. What was inside horrified me.

The paper read CAUSE OF DEATH: HEART FAILURE. I became physically sick and a feeling of being stabbed in the gut took over my body. All the pain I thought I had processed and healed resurfaced and shattered my spirits. Each time I tried to pull myself out of the pain, something would happen and all the peace I'd found would be lost.

There is no lasting peace without God at the center of my life. I knew that, if I could learn to surrender my pain to God, he would give me peace.

I also knew that sitting at home, staring at Faith's empty bedroom, only increased my insanity. And attempting to adjust to everyday routines was a huge challenge. But I knew I needed to get back to school as a step in my recovery.

Years before, when I'd been taking a public speaking course, a gentleman was sitting in class after experiencing the death of his daughter. I wanted to console him, but being a stranger, I retreated in silence. Maybe I acted out of fear or pride; either way, looking back, I realized I hadn't done the right thing. At the time, I wondered how he could be in school after losing his daughter. *If one of my daughters died*, I thought, *there is no way I would be sitting in class.* I kept asking myself, *How is he in school right now?*

Now it was my turn to find the strength and courage to sit in class after losing a child. Walking back into the class that first day with my head held low, I simply wanted to survive. I felt all eyes on me— every student and staff member knew I had just lost my daughter. Most people were sensitive to my trauma, and each had a unique approach to helping me. I could sense that people no longer treated me like they used to. People gave me hugs and words of encouragement, and I appreciated all their efforts to try and not make me feel like an outcast. When I made it to my seat, a student sitting nearby looked at me and asked, "How are you in school right now?"

Be Mad at God

There it was: A stranger was bold enough to ask the question, "How are you really doing?"—a question I was too scared to ask years ago. I simply answered, "I don't know." Getting my degree was no longer as important to me as it used to be. Just getting through the day was all that seemed to matter. How could I think about writing a term paper when all I want to do was write a goodbye letter to Faith? Answering my fellow student's question left me lost, but internally I knew God could teach me how to live again.

I would never know the miraculous things God could do if I hadn't invited God to do them. The miraculous things started with just getting out of bed. Each day my thoughts and emotions were scattered. Life around me kept going forward and I did not want to be a part of it. Despite my lack of interest in life, my wife and children kept loving me. It was this love that got me through those dark days.

When everything went wrong, God was right there. When I could not feel God's presence, he never left me. While driving one afternoon, I received a phone call from a family friend. Jim asked me how I was doing, and he let me share my anger, bitterness and confusion. Then Jim said something I will never forget: "Give yourself permission to be mad at God. God can take it." I wanted to trust what he said was true, but I was puzzled. I'd always believed you could not and should not be mad at God. I believed being mad at God was wrong. It was upsetting to think I could be mad at God, but if there was ever a time to be mad, this was it. And now I was being given permission to do just that.

I needed to know more. Jim asked, "Do your children ever get angry with you?" I said, "Yes, many times." Jim followed up by saying, "But you can handle it, right?" I said, "Of course I can handle it." Jim then asked, "Will your children always be happy with you?" I answered confidently, "NO! However, I will never stop loving my children no matter how mad they are at me." Jim said, "It's the same thing with God."

Jim asked, "If Jesse Cruz can take it, how much more do you think God can take when you are mad at Him?" He encouraged me to be mad at God. He said, "God understands you're mad and it's okay to be mad at Him. God doesn't expect you to be happy with him when you're in pain. God expects you to be human."

That conversation changed my relationship with God. As I released my anger with God, I shrieked in horror from what had happened to my daughter. I screamed and yelled at God. I sobbed and told God how mad I was with him. I demanded an explanation and an apology.

No matter how much I have felt hurt or disappointed by God, he has always been there to hold me and help me through my anguish. God kept giving comfort as a good father does. God still chose to love and accept me even when I felt unlovable and unacceptable.

Now, I give myself permission to be mad at God and I am honest about my emotions. No longer do I wait until I am mad to approach God. Any concern, fear or blessing I have leads me into a conversation with God.

Take Out the Trash

After Faith's death, it seemed like we'd ended up using her room as a storage room. Finally, there came a day when it was time to dig in and haul out the trash that had been piling up in her room.

So much of the stuff could not even be donated because of the condition. There was so much stuff, and the dumpster couldn't hold everything. The piles and piles of trash made it clear that we had lost control of our entire lives. Our yard looked like a garage sale gone wrong with all the stuff and the piles of trash around the dumpster. I had never been so excited about trash day. When the garbage company came the following day, they left without taking a single piece of garbage.

The garbage company didn't pick up our trash due to some mix-up on our account. Over the next few days, the pile kept growing. As the pile of junk grew, my patience was wearing thin. As the junk began to pile higher, my spirit and emotions started to drag low. With each new bag of garbage, I felt more discouraged that my life would never get cleaned up.

As I tossed another garbage bag on our unending trash pile, I paused and stared at all the stuff we were getting rid of. I thought decluttering stuff from my house would somehow declutter my spirit. I thought taking out the physical trash would eliminate the emotional baggage I had been carrying.

Garbage became symbolic of my life. I had never before looked at a pile of trash with such thought. My heart had become a landfill, piled up with the toxic waste of grief, and it was beginning to rot my soul. I had told myself I had released the pain and burdens to God, but I hadn't. I was still holding onto the pain. I kept thinking that if I let go of the last of the trauma surrounding Faith's short life, I would somehow be letting go of Faith's memory.

All the empty promises and unfinished love died with Faith, and with no place to distribute that love, I sabotaged my healing by staying trapped in an endless pity party. As the tears flowed down my face, I became determined not to allow the trash of my life to spoil my treasures.

Conversation with Myself

As I took time during all that was going on to do some journaling, I realized this:
I have become accustomed to pain, not just recently but throughout my life. I have taken pain, struggle and trauma on as my identity. Somehow it seems I needed this pain. Without the pain, I don't have a way of recording the memory of Faith. I know I should release the pain, but I'm hesitant. When all the pain is gone, I'm afraid that I will somehow lose myself and lose what is holding Faith and me together.

I'm trying to unload a small portion at a time. I need to remember pain is not my identity, but it is part of my story. It is not the entire book; however, it is an important chapter.

My heart will be forever shattered, and I am trying to sweep up the pieces. Those pieces seem to be all I have of Faith. I ask myself, *When will I find the courage to sweep those last of pieces pain away and realize that there is more to Faith and me than just the pain?* For now, I leave the dustpan in the other room. I know if I can be empowered to rid myself of the constant agony that follows me like a summer shadow, I will be able to heal.

Oddly, sitting here even now, as soon as I start to feel I am healing, a song starts playing and I am pulled back into the pain. Or there might be a smell, a building, a word heard, a sound, a color, a taste, or the look on someone's face, and I am instantly reminded of what happened in that NICU room. I now know to be strong is to be weak. I know I will always carry around pieces of this pain, hoping one day I can look at Faith's life not as an exit from me, but an entrance to our heavenly Father.

Faith is a Great Teacher

I am grateful for all the life lessons Faith taught me while in the hospital. Years later, I am still discovering how my daughter, Faith, taught me lessons about relationships. My relationship with my wife, my children and my friends are healthier than they have ever been. I was reminded of how limited our time is and learned to appreciate every moment spent with my loved ones. As Faith's parent, I thought it was my responsibility to teach her; instead, Faith taught me more about how to live than I ever could have taught her.

Some days my faith was in the valley, other times it was on the mountaintop. By keeping an open mind and heart, I felt ready to receive the challenging lessons God was attempting to teach me. God can and will use the most inspiring people you know, as well as the people you dislike the most, to help you grow. I was amazed to see Faith's impact on me and the world. How could it be that an infant who couldn't even speak could influence me more than most adults? My daughter whom you never met has impacted you because you are reading this book. Faith was one pound and unable to speak or even breathe without extensive support, yet she can influence others in amazing ways!

As you read this book, her influence and life can touch your life. Just when you think you aren't rich enough, strong enough, young enough, old enough, talented enough, blessed enough or have enough opportunities, just know that because you are God's child, you are ENOUGH! If my daughter can be a miracle for me and you, imagine what an impact you can have on others!

Strangers Will Change Your Life

Having a relationship with God provided us with supernatural insights during this crisis. I began talking with Desiré about all we had endured, and God spoke into her life by giving us both a revelation we would never forget.

Let me put the revelation into context. Haleigh's biological father died before he ever had the chance to meet his daughter. For most of Haleigh's life, I have been her dad. I know I'll never be her biological father and I can never truly replace him. I'm sure he would have been an amazing dad. It troubles me to know he'll never experience that special daddy-daughter relationship with Haleigh. I love Haleigh like my own and will continue to do so for the rest of my life. I'm the one she calls Dad, but I know my role as dad came from a tragic loss.

During a conversation with Desiré, she reminded me I had been raising another man's child for years. I am raising his daughter on earth while he is caring for my daughter in heaven—a complete role reversal, in effect. I know Haleigh's father celebrates eternity with Faith, while Haleigh and I celebrate our life on earth. It is comforting to know Haleigh's father is returning the favor and looking after Faith.

I believe everything that happens in life is connected. The suffering of a stranger can influence my family in some unknown way. Suffering for one person is suffering for all. We might not be directly impacted, but there will be an indirect effect. It is inspiring to know two people who have never met each other can play such an essential role in each other's lives.

HEALING FAITH

Who is the Better Father?

One morning, the spirit of the Lord convicted me with this question: "Do you think you are a better father than I am?" I'd been angry at God because I thought I could have given Faith the best life. Yet I failed to realize that even the most remarkable life on earth pales compared to what life in heaven is like. Up until then, I had believed there was no substitute for me as Faith's father. I was wrong. I know Faith is with the greatest Father of all time.

The hope of any Christian parent is to see their children in heaven someday. My feelings of missing Faith still bring me grief, but my heart accepts that her life is in the hands of the One who formed the earth. If I can remind myself that she's living in eternal peace, I can set aside my temporary emptiness.

Whether Faith lived for forty-two days or a hundred years, she will spend more time with her heavenly Father than she would have ever spent with me.

Dear Faith

My precious Faith, January 6 is here again—it is the hardest day of the year for me—and you are not here.

My healing has allowed me to accept all the things we will not do together. I decided to share this list not as a reminder but to let people know it is okay to share our hurts in a healthy way.

Faith, I will not hear your cry or put you in a onesie. I will not bundle you up and bring you home from the hospital. I will never change your diaper or bathe you. I will not watch you take your first steps. I will not be able to pick you up after you stumble. I will not hear you utter your first words. I will not be able to tuck you in at night or give you a goodnight kiss. I will never read bedtime stories to you. I will not see your smile. The sound of your laugh will never fill my ears. I will never hear you say "Daddy" or "I love you." We will not have our secret handshake. I will not coach any of your sports teams. I will not see you on your first day of school. I will never hold your hand when you are scared. I will not go on bike rides with you. I will not get to travel with you or go on hikes with you. I will never be able to cry with you. I will not be able to capture silly photos of us together on some wild adventures. I will never see you try to wear my shoes. I will never be able to check under your bed for monsters when you are afraid.

I will not sing or dance with you. I will not be able to bring you to church. I will not get to teach you about God's love. I will not be able to teach you the importance of kindness, generosity, honesty and respect. I will not be able to teach you about faith, hope and love. There will not be any trips to get ice cream on a hot summer day. I will not take road trips with you or watch you get your driver's license. I will not see you get your first job or witness you getting your first paycheck. I will not get to teach you financial responsibility. I will not see you go to prom or graduate. I will not see you go to college or begin a career. I will never be able to walk you down the aisle when you get married.

Pain with a Purpose

When I reflect on how our family came to be, I am astonished by how miraculous everything has worked together. My daughter Haleigh was brought into my life from the tragedy of losing her father. Mariah was brought into Desiré's life through the trauma of divorce. Desiré and I were brought together from two painful situations.

If I isolated all these events, our life would appear like a complete mess, a family full of disaster and dysfunction.

For too long, I looked at life from a microscope perspective. I realize I am often too close to see the bigger picture to understand the greater plan. I am learning that the greater plan for my life cannot be viewed entirely in the present moment. The current situation is often too new and fresh for me to have a clear understanding. Only when I pause and look back on my life do I recognize how each event has brought triumph.

Without all the craziness, the Cruz family would not even exist. This book would have never been written, and you would never have been able to join me on this journey of hope and healing. Without the pain I suffered, hope would not have been found. I am not happy about the pain from which this journey grew—it still hurts.

I now know I have a choice about what to do with the pain that enters my life. If I had chosen to live a hopeless life, the pain would have consumed me. Without the depth of the pain I experienced, I don't think I would have been fully introduced to God as the ultimate healer.

Each tragedy in my life seemed to be built upon the next tragedy and it's taken me years to label those events as lessons. Earlier in my life, I failed to realize that evaluated pain is one of the most helpful tools I could use in my faith journey.

Through the pains of my life, my purpose is being revealed. If just one of these events had not happened, then the equation of who I am and who my family is becoming would cease to exist. Pain has been one of my greatest teachers. The pain was the very thing I tried not to feel, yet it was what I needed to embrace the most to become the man and father I am today.

I thank God for receiving my daughter Faith. I still miss her, and my heart still grieves for her every day. Without Faith, I could never have fully become the father I am to Haleigh and Mariah. I would not have become the husband I am to Desiré. I would never have been able to share my story with you. From the depths of hopelessness, I learned about the greatness of God's grace.

Final Thoughts

During my time in the hospital and for several months after, I remained silent. I refused to talk about what I had witnessed. I bottled up my emotions even though I was shaken with despair and ready to explode. Refusing to speak about my painful story did not remove the chapter from my life. No matter how much I attempted to bury my grief, it resurfaced over and over. The more my silence persisted, the more violence inflicted my heart.

As Rick Warren has said, "Revealing your feeling is the beginning of healing." I will no longer allow my heartbreak to remain hidden. I will boldly speak about my wounds. I will free myself from the agonizing past, through God. If there is something tragic you have experienced, what will you do with your pain? Don't let it go to waste. Allow your pain to be the roadmap that brings healing to you and the world.

One of the greatest blessings you can give the world is your story. We admire the world-changers who make a difference and inspire us along the way. You are one of those people who can change the world. I want to encourage you to spread your light and your story and refuse to let darkness win.

An untold story never heals.

- Mary Demuth

I have shared with you the worst days of my life and all the awful details. My story is no greater than yours. Your story is unique. Understand that in the history of the world there has only ever been one YOU. If you share your story, it will change the world—I promise you. You are one decision away from the best decision of your life. Let your decision be to allow others to know your story fully.

I want to share a verse with you that has inspired me on my journey. 1 Peter 1:5–7 says, "Through faith you are kept safe by God's power. Your salvation is going to be completed. It is ready to be shown to you in the last days. Because you know all this, you have great joy. You have joy even though you may have had to suffer for a little while. You may have had to suffer sadness in all kinds of trouble. Your troubles have come to prove that your faith is real. Your faith is worth more than gold. That's because gold can pass away even when the fire has made it pure. Your faith is meant to bring praise, honor and glory to God. This will happen when Jesus Christ returns."

I believe we all have faith in something or someone. The faith we cling to each day can be strengthened and become more real when under pressure. Despite the hardships you encounter, keep the faith. Your troubles and tragedies do not disqualify the existence of God— they highlight the need for him. The more suffering there is in your life, the more you have a reason to seek out God as the solution. Every time you pass the faith test, God is glorified. When you feel like you are losing your faith, find your hope in God.

Your suffering is temporary. Your healing is eternal. No matter how far you fall into despair, God will raise you up. How marvelous it is to know God has allowed each of us to be part of his everlasting peace and joy. Never let go of what God has promised to give you: His eternal love.

About the Author

Losing Faith Finding Hope is Jesse Cruz's second book. His first book, *Live Your Dash-Discovering the 8 F's to Freedom*, has been widely received and has led to opportunities to live his passion of inspiring others to live life fully. Losing Faith Finding Hope is the fulfillment of a promise Jesse made to his daughter Faith.

Jesse is a Motivational Speaker, Coach, Youth Advocate, and U.S. Army Veteran. He lives in upstate New York with his wife, Desiré, and daughters Haleigh and Mariah.

Coach * Speaker * Author

Jesse knows the importance of choosing the correct speaker. The right one sets the stage for success and the wrong one for disaster. Jesse's authentic approach, combined with his rich storytelling ability, positions him as the top choice for many businesses and organizations. Jesse works directly with clients to bring a unique and impactful message to each experience.

To begin the conversation, visit
JesseCruzSpeaks.com

Made in the USA
Middletown, DE
30 April 2021